Issues in the Social Scie

Series Editor: An

Cont_xts

In the Same Series

Cont_xts: Media, Representation and Society

*Papers from a Conference held at
the University of Chester,
November 2006*

Edited by Meriel D'Artrey

Chester Academic Press

First published 2008
by Chester Academic Press
University of Chester
Parkgate Road
Chester CH1 4BJ

Printed and bound in the UK by the
LIS Print Unit
University of Chester
Cover designed by the
LIS Graphics Team
University of Chester

A catalogue record for this book is available
from the British Library

ISBN 978-1-905929-68-9

CONTENTS

CONTRIBUTORS

Dr Adrian Barton is Associate Dean (Graduate Affairs) in the Faculty of Social Science and Business at the University of Plymouth, where he has been employed since 2001. Prior to that, he was a lecturer in Criminal Justice Studies at the University of Glamorgan. Adrian's research looks mainly at the areas where health welfare and criminal justice touch, specifically drug and alcohol policy and child abuse. He has published widely in these areas, authoring two books and a number of journal articles. He is currently working on a British Academy funded project which examines the use of alcohol screening tools in a custody setting.

Dr Mark J. Bendall, following a First and PhD from Cambridge University, has published with US and UK publishers, including Fitzroy Dearborn (2001), Bowling Green University Press (2001), Greenleaf (2004) and Chester Academic Press (2006). His piece on Stakeholders and Corporate Social Responsibility appears in *Communication and Corporate Social Responsibility,* edited by Stephen May, Oxford University Press (2007).

Eclectic, integrated research focuses on representation and responsibility, spanning the fields of communications and criminology.

Mark is collaborating on a project on luxury and ethics with members of the United Nations Research Institute of Social Development, commencing a "Reading Bond" project and contributing to studies of pedagogy.

Dr Lisa Blackman is a Senior Lecturer in the Dept of Media and Communications, Goldsmiths, University of

London. She has published three books: *Hearing Voices: Embodiment and Experience* (Free Association Books, 2001); *Mass Hysteria: Critical Psychology and Media Studies* (with Valerie Walkerdine: Palgrave, 2001); and *The Body: The Key Concepts* (Berg, 2008). She is currently completing a book, *Immaterial Bodies: Affect, Relationality and the Problem of Personality*, and is one of the co-editors of the journal *Subjectivity*, published with Palgrave.

John Harrison is Senior Lecturer in Criminology at the University of Teesside and his research interests include the resettlement of offenders following release from custodial sentences, and surveillance and social control. He has published articles on prison and the support provided to prisoners on release and was involved in the development of the prisoner passport, a project aimed at resettlement. He has also been involved in the evaluation of intensive supervision programmes and is currently examining levels of resistance to the increasing level of surveillance in contemporary society. He is the co-author of *Study Skills for Criminology* (Sage, 2005).

Dr Ian Law is Reader in Racism and Ethnicity Studies at the University of Leeds. His primary research interests are in the conceptualisation and analysis of racism and ethnicity in various public policy contexts, which are examined in his recent books, *Institutional Racism in Higher Education* (Trentham 2004 with Phillips and Turney), *Race in the News* (Palgrave 2002), *Racism, Ethnicity and Social Policy*, (Prentice Hall 1996). Other major collaborative works include *Local Government and Thatcherism*, (Macmillan 1990) and *The Local Politics of Race*, (Routledge 1986). His research has addressed a range of themes including: the historical development of white racism; the changing nature of violent racism; the operation of institutional racism; the representation of race in news media; the politics of racism, ethnicity and migration; the problems and possibilities for achieving racial and ethnic equality across a range of public policy and private sector contexts; and innovative development of related forms of policy and organisational intervention. He is the founding Director of the Centre for Ethnicity and Racism Studies and he supervises a research programme which examines these issues in political discourse, the media, housing, social security and a variety of other social welfare arenas.

Dr Darren G. Lilleker is Senior Lecturer in Political Communication at the Media School, Bournemouth University and Director of the Centre for Public Communication Research. His research focuses on the ways in which politicians interact with society and citizens. Recent publications include *Political Marketing: A Comparative Perspective* (Manchester University Press, 2005), *The Marketing of Political Parties* (Manchester University Press, 2006), *Voters or Consumers* (Cambridge Scholars Publishing, 2008) and *Key Concepts in Political Communication* (Sage, 2006), as well as a number of journal articles. Dr Lilleker is also Chair of the PSA Political Marketing Group.

Dr Paula Wilcox is a Principal Lecturer in Criminology at the School of Applied Social Science, University of Brighton. She is a feminist researcher and activist who has written extensively on gender-based violence. Recent publications include *Surviving Domestic Violence: Gender, Poverty and Agency* (Palgrave Macmillan, 2006) and "Survivors of domestic violence, community and care", in S. Balloch & M. Hill (Eds.), *Care, Community and Citizenship: Research and Practice in a Changing Policy Context* (Policy Press, 2007).

Meriel D'Artrey (editor) is Deputy Head of the Department of Social and Communication Studies at the University of Chester and teaches on the Communication Studies, Public Relations and Criminology programmes. She has worked in corporate communications, advertising, marketing and public relations, both in-house and in agencies. She gained her MA from the University of Edinburgh and MSc from the LSE, and also has a PGCE in Higher Education. She has taught public relations in a number of universities. She co-wrote a chapter in R. Tench & L. Yeomans (Eds.), *Exploring Public Relations* (FT Prentice Hall, 2006). Her research interests include the interface between employment and education and, more recently, attitudes towards road safety issues.

FOREWORD

What can be said about the mass media that has not been said already? As the media themselves endlessly recycle the formats and contents of their merchandise, borrow brazenly from each other in order to sustain a myth of newness and relevance, so the study of media texts, images and institutions endlessly whirls around itself in a Dervish dance to the tune of social scientific productivity. Do the media encourage violence? Do the media sway voters' political choices? Do the media misrepresent major social events? Do they demonise some social groups? Do they shape our view of the world? Do they manufacture consent to the rule of capitalism? The social scientific answer to all of these questions has been consistently "yes and no". There is clearly some kind of relationship between mass media and social norms, but exactly what that relationship is has eluded a definitive answer for the best part of a century. From interest in the impacts of propaganda following the Great War, through studies of fascism, authoritarianism and media (mis-)use in the run-up to the Second World War, to the media effects models of 1950s (American) "mass society", to the "dominant ideology" debate of the 1960s and 1970s and the intense interest in texts, signs and symbols that followed in its wake, the media have been a fertile, if reliably ambivalent, field of research and scholarship for generations of academics. Indeed, any future historian seeking to understand the mass media in the twentieth century through social scientific writings about them might conclude that they started off as tools for propaganda, then became instruments of authoritarian rule, then vehicles for directing behaviour, then ideologically coded messages to secure political acquiescence, then a febrile bed of confusing voices each of which clamoured for attention in an overcrowded market place. Our historian might conclude from such a survey that social scientists were probably as baffled by the media at the end of the twentieth century as they were at the beginning.

Given the voluminous social scientific output on the topic, it is worth reminding ourselves that all these books and articles and essays are themselves "media", governed by rules determining what is and is not acceptable writing, what counts as evidence, what is a valid argument and so on. They may not be as "mass" as television, but there are many more than anyone could read in a lifetime and their formats and contents are as constrained and directed as anything you find on the flickering screen. Academic writing on the media is as much a part of the "hall of mirrors" (see, for example, Ferrell, Hayward & Young, 2008) in which our culture endlessly reflects itself as any message transmitted directly into our living rooms. In this case, any serious student of the media should read writings about them through multiple lenses; for such writing tells us something not just, or even primarily, about the media themselves, but also about the wider social issues that occupy our culture and our society at a given point in time. It tells us about the key intellectual problems that are occupying social science in particular and about important cultural tensions that are fuelling political and social debate in general. When social scientists debate media contents, formats, technologies, controlling institutions and so on, they are not (or should not be) scrutinising a strange specimen in a sterile laboratory. They are digging into the social fabric itself in order to try and understand social identities and divisions, political fault-lines and ideological currents. The media are part of our society, not something beamed into it from the outside. The study of the media is always at the same time the study of the society in which those media exist.

Foreword

In answer to my own opening question, then, the answer is that there is probably very little that can be said about the media that has not been said already. But there is plenty yet to say about the social and cultural contexts in which those media operate and about the cultural articulation of meanings, symbols and myths that they facilitate. In fact, all the best writing on the media tells the reader more about context than content. After all, there is an endless stream of commentary on "what's on" (or "what was on last night/week/month/etc.") the television, cinema, theatre; who wrote what book (including its "digested read"); why such and such a journalist got it completely right/wrong; and anything and everything else the media does. There is nothing short of a deluge of writing about media contents. But finding something that puts those contents in their proper place is a much rarer treasure and is something that anyone who considers her- or him-self to be a student of social life ought to seek out. Our ways of understanding things, as Lisa Blackman points out in this volume, are "historically contingent and therefore mutable"; but only if you understand the contexts that provide the contingency in the first place. So do not look to this book for definitive answers to what the media does or does not do to our behaviour, beliefs or values. Do look to it for insights into how the analysis of the media can be used to illuminate pressing social questions about identity, risk, surveillance, political representation, family violence, racism and anti-racism and gender troubles.

Martin O'Brien
University of Central Lancashire
October 2008

Reference

Ferrell, J., Hayward, K., & Young, J. (2008). Media, representation and meaning: Inside the hall of mirrors. In J. Ferrell, K. Hayward, & J. Young, *Cultural criminology: An invitation*. London: Sage.

ACKNOWLEDGEMENTS

With grateful thanks for the work undertaken by Dr Wainer Lusoli while he was a colleague at the University, and to Dr Katherine Harrison, also at Chester, who advised on the final editing.

Meriel D'Artrey

INTRODUCTION

The play on the word "cont_xts" in the title of this collection of conference papers illustrates some of the intrinsic complexities of the subject. It makes subtle suggestions of post-disciplinary linkages; of linguistic development and usage; intimations of genre, discourse and narrative; and a playful recognition of the needs of more recent stakeholders in the debate: the members of the texting society. Current media inter-t_xtual (*sic*) and cultural references acknowledge the influence of such media productions as *Big Brother* and *The X-Factor*, of celebrity culture, of the rapidly developing and paradigm changing social networking sites, and of the dynamic and contemporary nature of commentary on representation, as well as of the representation itself. There is general agreement that we live in a "mediated world" (Borchers, 2002, p. 5). There is less agreement over the influence and effects of the media. Revisionist developments in new media challenge traditional models of communications and undermine the old reductionist concepts, such as those of linearity or space. In fact, Ang (1999) argues for a complete rethink of communication theory to take account of these paradigm shifts.

The debate continues over the power of the mass media set against the power of the user, and issues of social responsibility set against media partisanship (sometimes subject and campaign–based, and often for commercial reasons). There are also many varying methodologies, inter- and post-disciplinary, attempting to qualify, quantify, or adequately decode and deconstruct the various interlocking strands. The theoretical underpinnings of the media therefore remain hotly contested, often on deeply held ideological and political

1

grounds. The discussion is not one which remains at the level of individual media texts, but rather has wide-ranging social and cultural implications.

Meyer (2002, p. xvii) argues that: "Our current state of knowledge certainly entitles us to conclude that the rules of the media system now dominate the political sphere". Many of the debates which come into the public sphere through the media, such as those on the effects of sex and violence in the media and on the linkage between media and crime, may detract from the real issues at stake, as the debate becomes focused on mediation itself. It may even be that the media make social problems seem glamorous through the use of spectacle and carnival. Jewkes (2004, p. 29) talks of: "large-scale ritualized joyriding", and Holmes (2005, p. 31) of the: "system of images [that] transforms the mundane into a hyper-real carnival of totemic monuments through which the 'masses' achieve congregation". Behind this apparent pantomime, of course, real people are dying. The growth in cultural criminology evidences this fascination with the theatre of crime.

Finally, while the topic seems to link primarily with issues related to news media texts, in fact wider cultural forms of mediation have implications for us all. It can be argued that the trajectory of these papers moves from an analysis of a specific media text to the conclusion that everything (including ourselves) is mediated. In fact, the whole basis of our political system is put under scrutiny, from the role of the individual voter through to those in power, with some of the fundamental precepts of our democracy challenged by the very issues these chapters address.

The chapters, part of a sequence of annual conference papers aimed both at students and at the academic community, attempt to "get under the skin" of these discussions. The addition in the title of the words "media, representation and society" to the already multi-layered concept of "cont_xts" introduces further potentially extensive and complex debates, not least in terms of how these strands are interwoven. Finally perhaps, the sheer importance of this subject area needs highlighting. Many of these papers deal with very real and pertinent issues. As Dyer suggests in *The Matter of Images*: "representations here and now have very real consequences for real people" (Dyer, 2002, p. 3). The papers address political representation, domestic violence, racism, mental health stigmatisation, surveillance, sexuality and drug use. There can be little doubt about the raw human content of these stories and about the importance of understanding better the role of media, representation and society in the early 21st century, faced with the challenges of victimisation and misrepresentation, or indeed disenfranchisement. In the wake of the recent disasters in both Burma and China, the extensive media coverage of the latter (enabled by the Chinese government inviting in the media) has directly contributed to the disparity in donations, and in effect to the saving of lives. The cynic might relate this new relationship with the media to pre-Olympic objectives of reputation management. Therefore, these discussions do not just exist in a conceptual sphere.

The terms of reference of the papers suggest a remit, drawing on McQuail (2000), which is both social scientific in approach, dynamic and pluralist, sweeping widely across perspectives, as well as contextual and normative. Taken as a whole, the papers address and develop a range of themes which are then, in the individual submissions, applied and tested within more tightly defined theoretical and practical parameters. Each paper draws on its own theoretical basis for discussion, emphasising the post-disciplinarity of this subject area. Few subject areas can offer such a wide remit and such an open canvas. Every lay person has a view, and every view will have some validity and go towards building the body of knowledge and understanding. Few will not have been affected by the issues raised in this collection, given that they go to the very root of our role as individuals within our society. That is what makes this such a fascinating and relevant area, and also such a difficult one to deconstruct.

Darren Lilleker, in his keynote paper, presents the current political landscape as one which would be familiar to the branding and marketing experts, using the "marketisation politics" as his paradigm. In his consumerised society, he identifies a disconnection between the represented (the voter consumers) and their representatives, a space filled by the media both as a positive and a negative force, and possibly an essential and pivotal one. The word "representation" once more takes on several meanings. He sees social marketing tools as offering an opportunity to create genuine dialogue across and within the political sphere: "a visible link between participating and being represented". The urgency within his paper is based on the risk to the basic tenets of our democracy if the voter is diminished in the face of the elected representatives. His contribution provides an overview of a political landscape which acts as a backdrop to the other papers.

Ian Law's paper takes the case study of the representation of the "complex character of racism" as a means of illustrating a number of key themes which other papers in this collection also address, and in so doing presents us with the same challenges for intellectual analysis as the media faces. The dual role of the media, on the one hand as a shaper of views (and therefore having the responsibility of the opinion-former) and on the other as a partaker in the fight against racism (and therefore partisan) – positions which could be at one and the same time a conflict of interest and/or consistency – is one such challenge, according to Ian Law. Paula Wilcox's paper on domestic violence also highlights this binary role. She draws on Evans (2001) to suggest that journalists are "both products of and participants in the society they seek to inform". Ian Law describes this role as ambivalent and controversial, both "privileging and silencing themes". Adrian Barton, in the context of the media representation of drug use, sees the role of the media as actually "reducing our capacity for informed debate and meaningful policy change". In each of the papers, the media plays different characters, sometimes benign and sometimes malignant, but always contextual and situational, taking part as it were as one of the characters. Tench and Yeomans (2006) draw some linked conclusions for the "public interest" from the contemporary "new global media environment", which include "increased insecurity and risk and greater ethical dilemmas" (chap. 4, p. 73). John Harrison's paper on the part played in this landscape by surveillance, which increasingly forms part of the normal default situation, highlights perhaps a more sinister role on the part of the authorities or the powerful, including the media. In fact, the contemporary paradigm of surveillance is even more all-pervading, as we also survey others.

Where Ian Law looks at race, Paula Wilcox takes domestic violence as her canvas, to investigate the media as "primary cultural site". She deconstructs the print media's constructions of domestic violence ("minimal and distorted") and suggests that her analysis might be used to explain how crime more generally is constructed. Her main criticism is the paucity of gendered analysis, which results in a lack of focus on the (usually) male perpetrators, the emphasis on the physical to the exclusion of other forms of domestic violence, and on the dominant individualistic approach, in which the victim can be held responsible. Paula Wilcox also highlights the essential newsworthy aspects of the reportage for the commercial survival of the media, which informs the dominant discourse.

Lisa Blackman provides an historical perspective on the experience of stigma, discrimination and prejudice for those with mental health problems, set against their representation in mainstream films. The paradox she highlights is that even a sympathetic portrayal can fuel moral panics, based on a fear of the unpredictable and irrational and running counter to attempts by mental health charities to quell prejudices. Once again, as with the domestic violence and race chapters, we have victims without a voice and we have a media fulfilling a paradoxical role. In this instance, the media is portrayed as an important site for "both changing people's minds and promoting fear and prejudice". Positioning mental health as akin to any other form of illness has, according to Lisa Blackman, led to sufferers being seen as "unable to control their behaviour". Once again, she finds "gendered differentiations" in the representation of the mentally ill, though dependent on the biogenetic paradigm. She points to the underlying stories of the individuals that would show the representations up as contingent and changeable. These "ghostly hauntings of stories never told" are not, in Lisa Blackman's view, adequately told through the genre of Hollywood films and through a constructed and framed narrative.

Adrian Barton's research into the framing by the media of illicit drug use as "fairy tales for the early 21st century" highlights again the role played by the media in shaping our perceptions and indeed, he suggests, "the cultural discourse". The paper sets this hypothesis within its historical as well as its contemporary context, tracing the normalisation of illicit drug use. The fairy tale settings presented by our tabloids bear little resemblance to the reality of the lives of most of our illicit drug users. The homeless street dwellers are unlikely to identify with Kate Moss and her glamour world. There is, too, a sinister angle to this, as Adrian Barton identifies the simplistic nature of reporting which "obscure (s) the complexities of drug use". He is suggesting that the British tabloid news media represent drug use as a morality tale for the 21st century, preventing engagement with the actual social issues. Barton might also have been referring to Amy Winehouse, where the public narrative obscures the private grief.

There is a similar sinister undercurrent when John Harrison talks of the "dreamlike state" in which we drift into a surveillance society. His underlying theme, though, is of an Orwellian nightmare that is as far from innocence as Adrian Barton's fairy tales; similarly, we are aware of the complex discourses underpinning such tales as those of Hans Christian Anderson or Aesop. His stage set is one where the watchers are themselves being watched. Surveillance is as relevant to discussions about specific media texts as it is to the wider debates broached in these papers.

Perhaps it is Mark Bendall's paper on the enigmatic and paradoxical Crisp which best highlights the multi-layered nature of the themes touched on in these papers and moves furthest from analysing media texts to the total mediation of identity. Crisp presents himself through multiple representations. It would be hard to know which of them is the "real" Crisp because, of course, no such thing exists. Crisp is merely an exaggerated version of our own multi-layered images and identities. He does, however, in a link back to the other papers, mediate his identities through media texts, such as magazine interviews and, indeed, interviews with academics.

If anything shouts louder from these pages than the

collected ideas of these academics, it is the voices of the victims, the forgotten, the "other". These papers raise as many issues as they resolve. That is the nature of a dynamic and controversial area of study. We hope that the reader will find in them a basis for further research and discussion and that, as such, they will have contributed to the debates which evidence both the vibrancy and the uncertainty of the 21st century media representation and societal landscape, embracing the chaos which Ang (1999) refers to.

References

Ang, I. (1999). In the realm of uncertainty: The global village and capitalist postmodernity. In H. Mackay & T. O'Sullivan (Eds.), *The media reader: Continuity and transformation* (pp. 366-384). London: Sage.

Borchers, T. A. (2002). *Persuasion in the media age.* Boston, MA: McGraw-Hill.

Dyer, R. (2002). *The matter of images: Essays on representation.* (2nd ed.). London: Routledge. (Originally published 1993).

Evans, L. (2001). Desperate lovers and wanton women: Press representations of domestic violence. *Hecate, 27* (2), 147-174.

Holmes, D. (2005). *Communication theory: Media, technology and society.* London: Sage.

Jewkes, Y. (2004). *Media and crime.* London: Sage.

Introduction

McQuail, D. (2000). *McQuail's mass communication theory.* (4th ed.). London: Sage. (Originally published 1983).

Meyer, T., with Hinchman, L. (2002). *Media democracy: How the media colonize politics.* Cambridge: Polity Press.

Tench, R., & Yeomans, L. (Eds.). (2006). *Exploring public relations.* Harlow: FT Prentice Hall.

9

POLITICAL REPRESENTATION & DEMOCRACY: WHAT IS WRONG WITH THE POLITICAL PUBLIC SPHERE?

Darren G. Lilleker

It is widely argued that there is a crisis in public communication: the public are not engaged in discussions of politics and public affairs, there is a decrease in participation in the electoral process and a collapse in engagement with the institutions of democracy. While these factors do not signal the inception of an introverted, introspective and self-centred society with little care for wider issues or concerns, it does indicate a problem exists for democracy. There appears to be a disconnection between the represented and their representatives, and hence democracy is seen as important, but is perceived to be functioning badly (Gerodimos, 2004). This paper explores the reasons for this, and in particular the key actors that academic literature claims to be at the centre of the problem – political actors, media commentators and the voter-consumer – before offering indications of how the problem may be solved. Prior to an analysis and discussion of the issues, however, it is useful to outline the underlying concepts and the nature of democracy and to ask why and how the key actors play a role in the functioning of democracy in an ideal state.

Democracy and the public sphere

The first concept we are required to consider when embarking on the study of politics is democracy, the age old idea that we the people have power over the politicians that run the state on our behalf (Arblaster, 1987). The simple, or perhaps simplistic, notion is that we are each represented by a Member of Parliament who then acts on our behalf during debates and when determining the direction of public policy (Rush, 2001). Whether this has ever been true is highly debatable: a strong current of thought that runs through Parliament is the Burkean notion that those in power know best and act in the best interests of the state, without the need to refer back constantly to the public in order to decide what to say or how to vote (Ferber, Foltz & Pugliese, 2007). However, perhaps we should not consider democracy to be a moribund concept based purely on the conclusion that politicians represent abstract goals, as opposed to referring to the opinions of those whose votes secured their seat in the House of Commons (Rush 2001). Evidence suggests a strong synergy between the priorities of governments and challenger parties during elections, and those of the mass electorate as measured by opinion polls (Gaber, 2006; Lilleker & Negrine 2006); while this is a fairly blunt instrument for measuring the representativeness of the political system, it seems that public opinion is never totally ignored and that the general public mood, feelings and opinions all contribute to the mental melting pot when policy decisions are taken (Acton & Lilleker, 2004).

However, critics of our political system often point out worrying indicators of a lack of representation or even misrepresentation. Those of us who recall the "cash for questions" scandal that contributed to the collapse of support for the Conservative Party in the early 1990s fear that our elected representatives are more interested in personal advancement than the best interests of society (see Gay & Leopold, 2004, for an exploration); thankfully, however, such incidents are isolated and easily exposed. This suggests that, rather than simply being represented by the political classes, we also have an equally powerful actor working on our behalf: the media (Negrine, 1994; Curran & Seaton, 2003; Rawnsley, 2004), which is claimed to be both influenced by (Gauntlett, 2005), and have influential power over (Miller & Philo, 1999), its audience and broader society.

It is within this understanding of a liberal democracy that we are able to identify pluralism of voice, representation of multiple political viewpoints and the masses having some input into political debate (Moloney, 2006). It is impossible to avoid political debate if one regularly buys a newspaper, local or national, and watches news or current affairs programmes on television. Politics is one of the mainstays of news coverage and the various political editors will compact information into easily digestible narratives with some relish, though this can be linked to questions regarding the dumbing down of politics and the stifling of public debate (Slayden & Whillock, 1999; Temple, 2006). One will often find that the doyens of political reporting, the BBC's Andrew Marr and Nick Robinson, *The Times*'s Peter Riddell or the Mirror's Oonagh Blackman, all lay claim to a very important role, acting as a watchdog over the politician and ensuring that they do indeed act in the nation's best interests (see Curran & Seaton, 2003). In the context of this role, the media does expose all manner of indiscretions, it should discuss the intricacies of policy design and it will translate the complex language of politics and economics into how policies will affect the lives of individuals, examining how the public are represented by the government of the day. The importance of the media in performing these roles is suggested when such factors are used as indicators of the health of national democracy (Hallin & Mancini, 2004).

This description of the media and its relationship with political representation, however, suggests something of a democratic ideal. The politicians predominantly act as representatives, sometimes referring to public opinion, but mostly looking beyond the often narrow perspectives offered by the masses; the media, in turn, will be performing checks and acting as a counterbalance to government and party communication, asking the questions the masses would like to ask and providing the answers they need. Within this context, the public sphere should be vibrant, informed of the political issues of the day, and the public should feel able to discuss these issues with a sound level of understanding. Equally, the public should feel capable of making sound judgements when asked to participate in the democratic process, usually at times of elections or referenda. But is this true of the society in which we live?; and, if not, why not? This paper thus proceeds to consider the extent to which we are represented by both the political classes or by the media and assesses the health of the political public sphere. In particular, we consider the concept of a market orientation of government and the media, a behavioural shift that in theory suggests a greater level of synergy between these organisations and the public, but may actually be contributing to the weakening of the concept of democratic representation. Equally, we consider the consumerisation of society, by public communication, but also as a social phenomenon in itself.

Representation, the public sphere and a market orientation

While once anathema to one another, it seems that politics and marketing are becoming increasingly intertwined; or, at the very least, politics is becoming marketised and perhaps market oriented. The notion of marketisation can refer to a practice of incorporating concepts and tools of marketing into political behaviour (Lees-Marshment, 2001; Lilleker & Lees-Marshment 2005a): thus we hear of parties being brands, voters as consumers of a political product and political outputs being, in turn, equated with services. However, marketisation is not symbiotic with a market orientation. Marketisation can be used to describe the process by which an organisation, or indeed a sphere of activity, can appear to act in the same way as a corporate brand; in contrast a market orientation best describes a philosophical perspective adopted by an organisation, which means that it constantly ensures that consumers' needs, wants and aspirations are satisfied by the product they are offered. This suggests that the market, or consumer, usually through extensive qualitative and quantitative market research, informs every stage of the life cycle of a product: from initial thinking that informs design through to the product's creation, all marketing communication, the placement of the product for consumption and eventual delivery on promises. If one considers the process through which a party may develop its macro product, an election manifesto, or indeed each micro product, the single political initiative, one can overlay the procedure of product development (Lilleker & Lees-Marshment, 2005b). A larger question is whether one should equate such a process with corporate behaviour. While we can argue that marketisation takes place, in terms of borrowing tools of corporate behaviour to inform the tactics of a political party (Lilleker, Jackson & Scullion, 2006b), it is firstly very difficult to identify how the voter or consumer, or voter-consumer, informs the political organisation (Lilleker & Negrine, 2006); and secondly it is equally difficult to argue that political organisations place the voter-consumer first in formulating either policy or strategy (Lilleker, Jackson & Scullion, 2006a), or whether it would be responsible or tenable to do so (Rush, 2001).

Arguably, and in terms of representing the public, there is logic underpinning the marketisation of politics; that is, that those who were once deemed citizens, who took an active interest in politics, discussed the important issues, and acted for the good of society, are now voter-consumers. The voter-consumer transfers the perspective of the supermarket across their lives: they are individualistic, brand conscious, seek personal incentives for their behaviour and possess a clear notion of the concepts of "me", "us" and "them" (Gabriel & Lang, 1995; Lilleker & Scullion, 2008). The compartmentalisation of groups, and of who represents whom, means that these voter-consumers seek out benefits for the self from every decision, including voting, and so political organisations must direct their appeals to the emotional, selfish and egocentric sides of their nature. Thus the political organisations, in response to this shift in society, have begun to employ a range of techniques that are associated with the corporate brand: simple messages, politically bland but emotionally laden appeals to individual aspiration, as opposed to any collective benefits for society, and the promotion of personality and style (Scammell, 1995; Franklin, 2004). While satisfactory for much commercial advertising, the question is whether such tactics are appropriate or sufficient to reach out to voter-consumers who face a barrage of similar messages? Furthermore, does the use of these techniques add up to a market-orientation in which the voter-consumers are given what they actually want, particularly if that core desire is effective representation?

One eloquent argument is that academics have become obsessed with political marketing as an idea; that it is we who apply marketing concepts to politics which are responsible for this marketisation paradigm

(O'Shaughnessy, 2002). This can be highly persuasive; however, the problem is that marketisation is a reality. The backgrounds of senior political advisors such as Philip Gould, Lynton Crosby, David Hill or Maurice Saatchi are not steeped in political science, but marketing communication. They are not simply journalists turned media advisors, as were Joe Haines, Alastair Campbell or Bernard Ingham; they are experts in advertising and marketing who are brought in to support parties in responding to socio-political developments that have impacted upon their behaviour. The collapse of lifelong party loyalty, the disengagement from electoral politics and individualisation of politics towards single interest groups, and the fragmentation of media audiences have all led to parties becoming marginal to mainstream society and finding huge barriers when attempting to get their message across to the electorate (Lilleker, Jackson & Scullion, 2006b). Within this context, it is understandable for parties to have looked at society, looked to the organisations that are able to build up followings – brand loyalty, for example - and attempted to borrow from the techniques of high street brands such as Tesco or internationally renowned market leaders such as Adidas, and other brands that are part of our day-to-day environment: Apple, Heinz, Cadbury, Hewlett-Packard, the Arctic Monkeys; the list is endless. Political parties want the same recognition and similar positive connotations attached to their brand, and want to regain and retain loyal supporters who will follow them through the highs and lows.

But how does this relate to the concepts of democracy? Theoretically, some suggest, if a political party is truly market oriented, there will be far closer synergy between public opinion and party policy; as with a corporate brand, the party will produce that which is required by its market

(Lees-Marshment, 2001). One could reasonably argue that political parties, like corporate brands, should have a symbiotic relationship with the broad swathes of the society they represent. Arguably, this allows the parties to govern on the behalf of the people, underpinned by a sound understanding of their needs, wants and fears; this allows policy to provide that which society needs. This is not far removed from ideals of a liberal democracy, and it is also descriptive of the work of brands that supply the shoes, household goods, banking services, etc. that we all use. The broad question is, however, are political parties and their elected members actually in touch with society? Does their use of marketing make our political representatives in any way truly representative of society? The more persuasive arguments are on the negative side; that marketing has actually helped to divorce completely the fractured relationship between society and government, between the masses and the Westminster village (Coleman, 2003; Lilleker, Jackson & Scullion, 2006a; Savigny, 2008). The branding of the parties does not engage the public; the style of marketing communication increases distrust and the logic of marketing leads to the disenfranchisement of those voters who are not deemed important for a party to win an election. Therefore, there is an irony at the heart of the political process. The public may think and act like consumers, including within a political context, when we would expect them to act as citizens; yet when they are treated as consumers by politicians, they do not like the result. Is this a case of "we receive the politics we deserve" or are politicians misreading the public?

Political representation: Is the Commons a public house?

David Marquand (2004) powerfully argues that the logic of the market, as discussed in the works of Schumpeter (1983) and Downs (1957), influential in the 1950s and ´60s, is actually contracting the public sphere. He argues that the implementation and subsequent acceptance of neo-liberal economic imperatives limits the perceived range of choices within the political marketplace, and so the public feels disenfranchised and disengaged from the political sphere. This sounds very familiar, as the media continually tells us about disengagement and cynicism, if not disenfranchisement; the last two UK General Elections were overshadowed by discussion of turnout to a far greater extent than there was discussion of political differences between the contenders. But is it simply perceptions of limited choice or, in the words of one cynical voter: "it didn't matter how you voted, you knew a bloody politician would get in" (Lilleker, 2002, p. 85). If one refers to literature on corporate communication, then the communication of the organisation is seen as crucial for gaining trust and loyalty, building relationships and gaining feedback on behaviour. One influential model, which has been argued to be most suitable for a political context (N. A. Jackson, 2003; N. A. Jackson & Lilleker, 2004), is the notion of symmetrical communication (Grunig & Hunt, 1984). The notion of symmetry suggests that communication is two-way and horizontal between the producer and consumer, so the relationship is non-hierarchical and power is evenly distributed. Within this paradigm, communication can be conversational and so started by either side. This is theoretically attractive and compelling, but appears to contrast sharply with our experiences of political communication.

Most textbooks view political communication as being top-down, from the senders in the political sphere to the audience. Clearly, this limits our definition of political communication to that emanating from the political classes; however, in terms of representation, this is perhaps not only adequate, but necessary. The important point is that, within classic perspectives, little communication is bottom-up, from the masses to the political class. This contrasts sharply with the notion of a market orientation or, indeed, of adopting the tools of the corporate world. However, commentators note that what the political parties and governments have borrowed is not the philosophy of marketing, which puts consumer views first, but the principles of salesmanship; simply the most visible tools. So we find that political communication is not only top-down, but also highly persuasive in nature, designed to build brand impressions, enforce positive perceptions of the sender, reduce positive attitudes towards opponents and sell the sender as a sound leader, government, etc. (O'Shaughnessy, 2002). This leads us towards viewing political communication as purely persuasive; this may well be true, but it is in opposition to the notion of representation and anathema to the provision of information.

Politicians argue that they must be image conscious on a permanent basis (Ornstein & Mann, 2000). The UK Labour Party's long crawl from the political wilderness, where they languished owing to association with the "winter of discontent" in 1978-9 and the party's ideological lurch to the left following the collapse of the Callaghan Government, was one that was as much a fight against the media as it was a battle for voter support (Thomas, 2005). James Thomas documents the anti-Labour bias of the media throughout the 1980s, a bias that shifted only after

Black Wednesday and the collapse of the Conservative Party's brand image post-1992. The actions of the media, it is argued, has led political parties to engage in a permanent campaign for the hearts and minds of voters and media alike; so all communication is explicitly designed to manage perceptions of the party, perhaps relegating informing to a secondary status (see Franklin, 2004, for a review).

While not implicit in Philip Gould's semi-autobiographical discussion of the creation of New Labour, his analysis of what was wrong in the party was paralysis of their communication machine, an analysis he claims was shared by Peter Mandelson. The perceptions of the party as "too militant", "red", "loony" and associated with "Scargill" and "strikes" (Gould, 1998, p. 52) mirror the framing of Labour by a largely right wing press (Thomas, 2005, pp. 87-117); it was these perceptions Labour's reformers strove to break down and so it was necessary to win over a large section of the Fleet Street journalists (Jones, 2002, p. 364). This led them to reform communications to include "positive, proactive press relations" (Gould, 1998, p. 56) and to make "the influence of electoral opinion as their first priority" (Gould, 1998, p. 55). Such notions map well on to the concept of the permanent campaign as practised in the USA since Cadell's advice to President Jimmy Carter in 1976 (see Ornstein & Mann, 2000); the key being the prioritisation of short-termist, adversarial, persuasive campaigning throughout the electoral cycle. The introduction of such tactics brings us neatly to the main problem experienced by parties in the UK over the last decade: the excessive use of spin.

Peter Mandelson, in critiquing the trajectory of New Labour, argued that good media skills were unequivocally necessary, but that they had "been allowed to fall into disrepute through overuse, and misuse when in inexperienced or over-zealous hands" (Mandelson, 2002, p. xliv). Spin has become a synonym for political communication within the public consciousness, and spin in itself has some fairly damning associations; we perhaps think of Jo Moore's suggestion of "burying bad news" beneath the coverage of 9/11 as an example, though that was not exactly spin. However, it is a dirty word that tarnishes the image of politics. Is this accurate? Spin is not new. In fact, we all spin in terms of attempting to manage others' perceptions of us. We may not offer the real reason for being late; instead, we will invent unforeseeable and serious circumstances that prevented our timely arrival. Equally, attempts to hide bad news while promoting facts that make a government appear competent is not a feature of the Blairite era; it was also a feature of the work of Wilson's press advisor Joe Haines and Thatcher's media manager Bernard Ingham. However, the increased and greater strategic deployment of media management, both in terms of attempting to set the news agenda ("what is reported") and the frame ("how it is reported") caused a rift to occur between government and the journalists. This is described best by a self-confessed victim of Blair's media management machine, former BBC journalist Nicholas Jones. Jones (1996, 2002) argues that the lack of transparency within government, and perhaps what has now arguably become a feature of political parties generally, is fuelling public mistrust and encouraging disengagement from electoral politics. Again, this contrasts sharply with the notion of a market orientation and with our democratic ideal; the public may not know who or what they can trust and so reject all communication from political parties and disengage from the electoral democratic process.

The main problem that is raised by the political sphere is that there is a demand to act more like consumer brands; these well-rehearsed arguments hinge around the notions of consumer culture and the decline in political interest and voter loyalty. Equally, parties are driven to use media management by what they feel are an aggressive media; consider not just the negative Labour reportage of the 1980s, but media treatment of successive Conservative leaders prior to David Cameron's election. Therefore, spin is blamed upon the media; yet the media, as we will see, have a different perspective. The problem here is that there is a perception that the media is blocking messages from the political sphere to the public sphere; spin is a means for getting around this blockage. But perhaps this is not simply a problem with modern media management, but more a problem that resides at the heart of the development of the permanent campaign. By definition, campaigns are persuasive. If all parties do is campaign, with all the associated use of subterfuge, propaganda and gimmickry, and if our voter-consumers are aware of campaigning and sceptical of grand promises and sales techniques, perhaps it is no wonder that the message does not get through. The voter may well be susceptible to brand messages, often because of satisfactory purchase experiences. However, our experiences of political outputs tend to be mediated; so are our media watchdogs serving the public in cutting away the spin and revealing the truth? Can we find the public voice expressed by our media?

A plural media: Entertaining or informing?

Clearly, there are ways in which anyone can have a voice: citizen journalism, social networking tools, the increased use of blogs and wikis, allow us all to comment on any subject. But in terms of broader societal views, the media claims to act on behalf of the public, both in terms of airing public opinion and ensuring the government and political system is held to account in the name of the public good. These are highly complex, value-laden moral tasks; but are these tasks within the remit of our media? Rawnsley (2004) argues not; while critiquing political communication in general, his argument is that participatory democracy can only be reinvigorated by greater use of information communication technology, as the mass media are largely failing to inform the public or encourage democratic debate within the public sphere. This, however, is not a reason to blame the media for disengagement. Rawnsley argues that the political coverage has become democratised owing to the fragmentation of the media; it is instead the style and one-way direction of political communication that is the problem. While Rawnsley accepts that the public are constrained by systemic devices that lead for many to an inability to participate, he fails to discuss in great depth the ritualistic consumption of news that is argued to be the case for many people within society. This means that media audiences will pick up headlines from breakfast television, possibly one daily newspaper only and possibly an evening or nightly news bulletin (Gillespie, 2006). Few people are what Gillespie describes as cosmopolitan news consumers or strategic zappers; individuals who will tailor their news consumption to suit their individual needs. In fact, Gillespie's research only finds these people emerging at times of personal crisis and distrust of the usual news channel: British Muslims turning to Al-Jazeera during the Iraq War, for example. The argument that there is a political communication democracy, therefore, is seriously undermined by the limited news consumption of the average citizen, suggesting that the traditional role ascribed to the news media is still in demand within society, despite media fragmentation and increased access to information sources. Yet the mode of political reporting is often seen as the cause of disengagement; but in what sense can this be true?

The criticisms of the media for dumbing down political discourse, presenting a limited news agenda and packaging news within editorial frames appear to hold pertinence. But perhaps these criticisms are unfair. Pippa Norris's compelling findings from a cross-national study suggest that what some argue are the symptoms of dumbing down actually do the job the journalists suggest they do; as Temple (2006) suggested, they encourage interest in politics (Norris, 2000). Furthermore, the personalisation of issues and the conversion of highbrow political discourse into the language of the layman aid understanding of political information. This runs counter to the traditional theories of a media malaise from which the coverage of current affairs in politics can encourage civic disengagement, ignorance of political issues, disenchantment with the contenders for government and apathy and discontentment with the political process (Murdock & Golding, 1989; Dahlgren, 1995; Jones, 1996; Rosenbaum, 1997; Gunther & Mughan, 2000). Instead, Norris (2000) suggests that there is a virtuous circle in which a critical media encourages the public into "actively sifting, sorting and thereby constructing political impressions in line with their prior predispositions... [which] represents an iterative process gradually exerting a positive impact on democracy" (Norris, 2000, pp. 217-8). However, this thesis is problematic. Firstly, Norris admits that she cannot demonstrate a causal link between media criticism and civic engagement; this means that there is a certain amount of assumed causality underpinning the hypothesis. Secondly, and perhaps more crucially, these people are the same as Gillespie's cosmopolitan news consumers; the minority of active news junkies who seek both information and participation. If these are a minority and there is an increasing gap between the information rich and the majority who are information poor, this is, as Norris notes, a serious problem for representative democracy. Norris argues that we have a more educated citizenry, so possessing higher cognitive skills, who also have greater access to a range of information sources; therefore, they have the ability to choose how they are participating in politics. This raises a further problem.

Arguably, there are now far more individuals who have ritualistic patterns of information gathering, often ones that are limited; therefore, we cannot say with any clear certainty that there is a plethora of cosmopolitan citizens all participating in political debate. Furthermore, the fact that democracy rests upon participation, yet it is the democratic process that is being undermined by apathetic behaviour, suggests there is a problem. This fact leads us to the conclusion that the media cannot be absolved of all involvement in nurturing disengagement. But, despite the case developed thus far, can we actually find evidence that the media is not acting within its role as protector of the public interest and instead encouraging cynicism in political communication?

Concerns begin when considering the news values of any media organisation. The standard judgements that are made by editors when setting the news agenda for a newspaper or broadcast relate to: the organisation's ideological leaning, or loyalty to an idea or party; the status of characters involved in the story, and perhaps their proximity to high status personalities; the extent to which the editor feels news should be balanced, in terms of political party coverage, or the nature of news (political / gossip / sport); the space and time available; and the appropriateness of a story for the readership within the given context (Blumler & Gurevitch, 1995, p. 95). While the importance of these principles can all be recognised, we do not get the sense that providing important information is implicit in setting news values. Critics argue that often editorial bias is the most influential in determining the news values of a newspaper, though ensuring balance is equally argued to stifle debate on television. Yet greater concern is expressed regarding, not the overt political bias upon reporting, but the manner in which politics is reported. This means that stories that are easily attached to a personality or that highlight mistakes, transgressions or disagreements between personalities, and can be presented in an entertaining, engaging editorial style, gain greater coverage than stories that would be objective, informative and impersonal (see Lilleker, 2006a, pp. 138-9; also Blumler & Gurevitch, 1995; Donsbach, 1997). The concentration on certain types of stories, which fit with a perception of what the audience wants, means that there appears to be an accepted way political stories are framed, which arguably encourages audience interest in the story, but not in politics itself.

It is appropriate to consider an example here: the Blair-Brown battle for control over the Labour party, a saga that played out in the British media for about ten years. The narrative largely rests on unattributable off-the-record briefings, hints, possible suppositions, some of which have been reinforced by factual evidence, regardless of the truth, or the extent of the truth, behind the narrative; yet it is perhaps something that we all believe to be true. It is suggested a deal was done in the mid-1990s that gifted the Labour leadership to Blair and that Brown, perhaps the better contender, relinquished his rights in the name of the landslide victory Blair promised and delivered. Brown, meanwhile, got the second best job and used that position to attempt to steer the government's direction, so conflict occurred on various policies, most famously Britain's not joining the European single currency (EMU), and factions emerged around the two power bases. The conclusion to the story was the succession and the subsequent machinations of Blairites to undermine the less telegenic and troubled Brown. But the big question that should occur in relation to this narrative is: "So what?"

It is argued that, if there is conflict at the heart of government, it does not affect decision making in a quantifiable or indeed identifiable way; and that theoretically we can argue that conflict is a good thing, as decisions are questioned and there is no single faction around one person which controls decisions and sets the parameters for what is right or wrong. However, this is not how the narrative is framed and sold to media audiences. The conflict or debate surrounding the nation's possible entry to the EMU was described as a paralysis at the heart of government that affected our relationship with our European partners; furthermore, debate was focused on the patriotism of the Blairite faction which, with Mandelson as a key player, argued in favour of entry. This focus on the back story, what is occurring behind the scenes, as opposed to the actual events, was famously described as resulting from an obsession with process by Alastair Campbell; something he argued was damaging political engagement. Campbell's argument is, however, shared by academic critics of the media presentation of politics (for bibliography, see D. Jackson, 2008). The situating of political decision making into the discourse of the soap opera trivialises the democratic process and encourages the audience to be spectators rather than participants. In other words, audiences can equate the Blair-Brown feud with similar soap opera narratives: the

Mitchells versus Johnny Allen in Eastenders, the long-standing *Coronation Street* feud between Ken Barlow and Mike Baldwin; these are interesting and the audience want to see who wins, but they do not intrinsically care or see the importance of the outcome.

Such criticisms can be linked to various instances when the media is accused of dumbing down political debate; but what lies beneath this logic? Prominent journalists frequently argue that there is a requirement to make news entertaining, to translate the high language of politics into simple pictures that engage with the audience's everyday experiences, as well as selling copy to the public, and there are academic arguments that support this perspective (Temple, 2006). So there is a strong sense of a market orientation acting as a guiding hand over political reporting, the logic being that it must be attractive to the audience in terms of single items being entertaining, while the overall format of the news, the selection of content and the editorialising tone must attract audiences back in significant numbers. Across all the major broadcasters (except for the BBC) and the majority of newspapers, but particularly the tabloids, such constraints are a simple truism. The worry, however, is that, rather than audiences selecting their news on the basis of it providing what they need and supporting views they already hold, the ritualistic behaviour means that their access to alternative views of the world is severely limited and they are more susceptible to influence by the media than experiments tend to suggest. This is particularly the case when politics is viewed, not from a biased or single party political perspective, but cynically, suggesting that decisions are taken in an alien environment that has few connections with the real life experiences of the public. In other words, the processes that are discussed are seen as trivial bits of an ongoing soap opera, featuring a number of corrupt, power-hungry and self-serving individuals who may be entertaining to watch, but are unworthy of much consideration and not deserving of public support. Above all, politicians are seldom painted as public representatives; rather they often appear typecast as faction-driven and self-seeking. Such a narrative can only have a corrosive effect on democratic culture.

The public sphere: The consumerisation of society

The opening lines of Gabriel and Lang's portrait of modern society, *The Unmanageable Consumer* (1995, p. 1), argue that "the consumer has become a god-like figure, before whom markets and politicians alike bow". While the thesis does not discuss in depth engagement with political organisations or their messages, the authors do describe the interesting conundrum that, while organisations feel encouraged to be socially responsible owing to the rise of the activist consumer, the average voter appears to elect governments who offer low taxes and the opportunity for individual advancement (Gabriel & Lang, pp. 152-186). The impact of the neo-liberal philosophy and economic policies associated with the Thatcher-Reagan era is argued to have created a society of nihilists (Leys, 2001), who see little influence to be had by engaging in party politics, but who instead will participate in micro-politics: the issues that are seen as directly relevant to their lives (Keller & Berry, 2003, pp. 195-204). This emerging paradigm of a society founded purely on individualistic desires and social nihilism is seen as generally negative, in terms of its impact on democracy and ensuring both governmental and journalistic accountability and representativeness (Frank, 2000); yet the fact that these developments are argued to be as much market-driven, from below, as by the hegemony of the idea of consumerism as an ontology during the 1980s, is problematic. The question at the heart of this centres on whether society is a product of its politics, or if politics is a product of society; put simply, does society have the democratic system it deserves?

The reason for suggesting that developments in both political communication and journalism are market-driven is that, while it appears that disengagement has exacerbated in recent years, contiguous to marketisation, marketisation was in fact a response to voter dealignment and the fragmentation and postmodernisation of mass media audiences. Therefore, we hear of wide scale use of marketing and the introduction of a market orientation in order to reach the public; yet the public itself appears to move further away. In some ways, this is owing to the nature of marketised political communication and in others it could be the result of the media treatment of politics; however, we can also relate it in part to societal shifts that are independent of political communication.

The societal shifts are well documented and part of a wider evolutionary process. The breakdown of social cleavages defined by a rigid class structure had an attendant effect on party loyalty. The phenomenon of dealignment, in particular of the working class away from the Labour Party, was exacerbated by de-industrialisation, but more important for political engagement was the collapse of class consciousness. Gallie (1978) noted the rise of personal motivations as a driving force for political participation and voter choice, as opposed to more abstract collectivist ideals. Furthermore, this meant that parties that pursued policies built upon the interests of non-existent, stereotypical class members became an irrelevance, as did grand political meta-narratives and ideologies (Lilleker, 2002). One can argue that society began to outgrow grand narratives, or accept them as ideals only; alternatively one can argue that the current institutions failed to evolve with society as new ideals emerged during the 1960s (see Donnelly, 2005); however, without entering into debates on the historicism of social evolution, the key factor is that voters are increasingly unpredictable and are more likely to be driven by experiences as consumers than as citizens or voters (Scullion, 2008).

Yet these societal shifts, and their related attitudes and behaviours, are exacerbated, at the very least, as governments increasingly treat voters as consumers and elections as sales campaigns; when the media feature the masses in their consumer lives, or as consumers of political outputs; and when the media cater more for base instincts and desires than the provision of information, or access to the participation points that are required for active citizenship. This is certainly the perspective offered by Professor Stephen Coleman (2003) as he compares youth engagement with Westminster politics and the reality TV show *Big Brother*. While it would be spurious to argue that more young people vote in *Big Brother*, or similar reality shows, than at General Elections, because we do not know the frequency of voting by any one individual, it appears certainly to be the case that there is more engagement, interest and ego involvement in the outcome of reality TV contests than in contests that may decide who runs the country. The reason for this, we can suggest, is that it is possible to form attachments to participants in *Big Brother*, behaviour can be scrutinised to ensure that their actions match their rhetoric and there are gratifications to be earned by participating, having an effect on the result as well as the enjoyment of the process of participation. None of these activities appear possible in the case of Westminster politics. While Stephen Shakespeare's response to Coleman (in Coleman, 2003) highlights that similar machinations, posturing and alliance-forming occur in Westminster, these are not seen as "real" by media audiences; there is a lack of authenticity surrounding political actors. They are not seen as real people who share our life experiences and possess the same needs and fears, and so do not represent us symbolically, never mind politically. The public view of politics can, therefore, be considered as akin to Plato's famous cave analogy from *The Republic* (Plato, trans. 1977). The media offer shadows of Westminster life, framed within popular culture narratives; reality television, in contrast, offers real life in vivid technicolour.

What we find is that, overwhelmingly when the public discuss elected politicians, they talk of disconnection, and it is useful to talk about how citizens articulate their feelings on representation. Dean (2006) notes that the young generally lack trust in politicians, so any communication is viewed as less than credible and unworthy of much consideration. This, however, is not simply a problem for the young voter. Scullion (2006) found that his broader qualitative sample was equally disengaged and, in the context of a general election, "electoral encounters were overwhelmingly framed as interfering and imposing" upon their day-to-day lives. The roots of the erosion of trust are harder to identify, and are often the subject of assumption. It is convenient to blame the media and its obsession with the salacious; equally we can blame politicians who prove they are untrustworthy and are duly exposed by the media, and we could also blame the public themselves. It is argued that there is a general desire for stories about sleaze (Thompson, 2000), and a tendency to believe conspiracy theories and narratives of improper conduct among those who wield power; thus what we may well be witnessing is a spiral of mistrust. True, this is fuelled by the few occasions when politicians do not fulfil our expectations, and it is supported by narratives in the mass media (the circumstances surrounding the Hutton Inquiry or David Blunkett's private life) and popular culture (storylines in the BBC's *Spooks*, for example), but the origins are within the public as much as the media. The problem could be that it is easy to mistrust "others" with whom we have no understanding or connection. Hence, at the heart of this narrative of disconnection are notions of unfamiliarity between the representatives and those they represent.

Making connections?

The argument that there is a vicious circle in operation, with politicians and media spinning against one another and the public sidelined to be spectators of a Westminster soap opera, is well rehearsed in literature. The media can be identified as a barrier between politicians and the public, but then conversely it could be argued that the media also offers the sole point of connection. It may only show shadows of political life, but without television and newspapers we might not get any insights into the world of politics at all. Furthermore, an independent media commenting on politics and scrutinising the political process is desirable for a functioning democracy, so suggesting the media withdraw from politics would be to hinder, not enhance, democracy and a fully-functioning public sphere. Perhaps the public should be compelled to think more about politics, be less accepting of, and greedy for, dramatic narratives, and take a more active role in democracy. However, one can imagine the answer to such a campaign; the voter-consumer would surely ask what is in it for me and leave the minority to keep political debate alive. So perhaps we should turn to the political class and ask what can they do to draw voter-consumers towards them?

Research indicates that it not every citizen of Britain that mistrusts all politicians. Where there are points of connection, particularly at the constituency level, there is a strong sense of trust and loyalty (Lilleker, 2006b). The key reason is the strong sense of representation that occurs within certain constituencies, owing to the service offered. While this seems more likely to be a feature of democracy within constituencies where the contests are hardest fought and the margins tightest, there are some indications of satisfaction and engagement. Equally, some attempts are made to re-engage with some groups via the internet. WebCameron (www.webcameron.org) may offer fairly staged insights into the life of the opposition leader, many of which will be read as such by a media literate viewer, but it is intended to offer a more three-dimensional image of the man who is likely to be the next prime minister. More positively, some MPs are using social networks such as Facebook, a tool which can not only build connections between them and the ordinary citizen, but can also facilitate two-way interaction. This ideal form of communication could build a greater level of trust in politicians; however, it must be genuine and replicate offline, face-to-face communication, rather than being monologic or "question and answer" in format.

The importance of these ventures could be that it builds a connection between social network users and politicians; one which may not only build a relationship between two people, but a wider community through word of mouth. These connections into the Westminster village may mitigate against some of the most corrosive effects of cynical media narratives on the process and strategy of politics. In simple terms, politicians can no longer be treated as an "other" when they are also part of "us".

However, this cannot be realised by the sporadic use of Web 2.0 by a minority of elected representatives, so perhaps it may be a distant vision. However, the voter-consumer appears to want more than top-down heavily spun and mediated political communication. They want a return on their investment; basically, a visible link between participating and being represented. The media seems ill-equipped to make that link tangible, and the media-obsessed political communication machine seems unable to think beyond mass communication models. However, as the voter-consumer becomes more familiar with interaction between peers, employers and employees, students, teachers and lecturers, and commercial brands, a new communicative norm will be established. For politicians to come out of the "shadows" and be a member of "us" rather than "them", they need to consider how to make new information and communication technologies work for them and consider how to build a connection. It is on this connection that the future of representation and the political public sphere may well be built.

References

Acton, T., & Lilleker, D. G. (2004, September). *Listening to the public?: The influence of opinion polls on MPs.* Paper presented at the Political Studies Association's EPOP Specialist Group Conference, Oxford.

Arblaster, A. (1987). *Democracy.* Milton Keynes: Open University Press.

Blumler, J. G., & Gurevitch, M. (1995). *The crisis of public communication.* London: Routledge.

Coleman, S. (2003). *A tale of two houses: The House of Commons, the Big Brother House and the people at home.* London: Hansard Society.

Curran, J., & Seaton, J. (2003). *Power without responsibility: The press, broadcasting and new media in Britain.* (6th ed.). London: Routledge. (Original ed., 1981).

Dahlgren, P. (1995). *Television and the public sphere: Citizenship, democracy, and the media.* London: Sage.

Dean, D. (2006). View from the armchair: Why young people took no interest and no notice of the campaign. In D. G. Lilleker, N. A. Jackson, & R. Scullion (Eds.), *The marketing of political parties: Political marketing at the 2005 British general election* (pp. 231-50). Manchester, Manchester University Press.

Donnelly, M. (2005). *Sixties Britain: Culture, society and politics.* Harlow: Pearson Longman.

Donsbach, W. (1997). Media thrust in the German Bundestag election, 1994: News values and professional norms in political communication. *Political Communication, 14* (2), 149-70.

Downs, A. (1957). *An economic theory of democracy.* New York: Harper & Row.

Ferber, P., Foltz, F., & Pugliese, R. (2007). Cyberdemocracy and online politics: A new model of interactivity. *Bulletin of Science, Technology & Society, 27* (5), 391-400.

Frank, T. (2000). *One market under God: Extreme capitalism, market populism and the end of economic democracy.* New York: Doubleday.

Franklin, B. (2004). *Packaging politics: Political communications in Britain's media democracy.* (2nd ed.). London: Arnold. (Original ed., 1994).

Gaber, I. (2006). The autistic campaign: The parties, the media and the voters. In D. G. Lilleker, N. A. Jackson, & R. Scullion (Eds.), *The marketing of political parties: Political marketing at the 2005 British general election* (pp. 132-56). Manchester, Manchester University Press.

Gabriel, Y., & Lang, T. (1995.) *The unmanageable consumer: Contemporary consumption and its fragmentation.* London: Sage.

Gallie, D. (1978). *In search of the new working class: Automation and social integration within the capitalist enterprise.* Cambridge: Cambridge University Press.

Gauntlett, D. (2005). *Moving experiences: Media effects and beyond.* (2nd ed.). Eastleigh: John Libbey. (Original ed., 1995).

Gay, O., & Leopold, P. (Eds.). (2004). *Conduct unbecoming: The regulation of parliamentary behaviour.* London: Politico's.

Gerodimos, R. (2004, February). *Mind the gaps: Political rhetoric, executive reality and public trust.* Paper presented at the International Conference, 'Communication in the Age of Suspicion: Trust, Communication and Culture', Centre for Public Communication Research, Bournemouth.

Gillespie, M. (2006). Transnational television audiences after September 11. *Journal of Ethnic and Migration Studies, 32* (6), 903-21.

Gould, P. (1998). *The unfinished revolution: How the modernisers saved the Labour Party.* London: Little, Brown.

Grunig, J. E., & Hunt, T. (1984). *Managing public relations.* New York: Holt, Rinehart and Winston.

Gunther, R., & Mughan, A. (Eds.). (2000). *Democracy and the media: A comparative perspective.* Cambridge: Cambridge University Press.

Hallin, D. C., & Mancini, P. (2004). *Comparing media systems: Three models of media and politics.* Cambridge: Cambridge University Press.

Jackson, D. (2008). Citizens, consumers and the demands of market-driven news. In D. G. Lilleker & R. Scullion (Eds.), *Voters or consumers: Imagining the contemporary electorate* (pp 141-61). Newcastle: Cambridge Scholars Publishing.

Jackson, N. A. (2003). MPs and web technologies: An untapped opportunity? *Journal of Public Affairs, 3* (2), 124-37.

Jackson, N. A., & Lilleker, D. G. (2004). Just public relations or an attempt at interaction?: British MPs in the press, on the web and 'in your face'. *European Journal of Communication, 19* (4), 507-33.

Jones, N. (1996). *Soundbites and spin doctors: How politicians manipulate the media – and vice versa.* (New ed.). London: Indigo. (Original ed., 1995).

Jones, N. (2002). *The control freaks: How New Labour gets its own way.* (New ed.). London: Politico's. (Original ed. 2001).

Keller, E., & Berry, J. (2003). *The influentials.* New York: Free Press.

Lees-Marshment, J. (2001). *Political marketing and British political parties: The party's just begun.* Manchester: Manchester University Press.

Leys, C. (2001). *Market-driven politics: Neoliberal democracy and the public interest.* London: Verso.

Lilleker, D. G. (2002). Whose Left?: Working class political allegiances in post-industrial Britain. *International Review of Social History, 47* (Suppl.), 65-85.

Lilleker, D. G. (2006a). *Key concepts in political communication.* London: Sage Publications.

Lilleker, D. G. (2006b). Local political marketing: Political marketing as public service. In D. G. Lilleker, N. A. Jackson, & R. Scullion (Eds.), *The marketing of political parties: Political marketing at the 2005 British general election* (pp. 206-30). Manchester: Manchester University Press.

Lilleker, D. G., Jackson, N. A., & Scullion, R. (2006a). Conclusion: Was 2005 the year political marketing came of age? In D. G. Lilleker, N. A. Jackson, & R. Scullion (Eds.), *The marketing of political parties: Political marketing at the 2005 British general election* (pp. 251-64). Manchester, Manchester University Press.

Lilleker, D. G., Jackson, N. A., & Scullion, R. (2006b). Introduction. In D. G. Lilleker, N. A. Jackson, & R. Scullion (Eds.), *The marketing of political parties: Political marketing at the 2005 British general election* (pp. 1-30). Manchester, Manchester University Press.

Lilleker, D. G., & Lees-Marshment, J. (2005a). Conclusion: Towards a comparative model of party marketing. In D. G. Lilleker & J. Lees-Marshment (Eds.), *Political marketing: A comparative perspective* (pp. 205-28). Manchester, Manchester University Press.

Lilleker, D. G., & Lees-Marshment, J. (2005b). Introduction: Rethinking political party behaviour. In D. G. Lilleker & J. Lees-Marshment (Eds.), *Political marketing: A comparative perspective* (pp. 1-14). Manchester, Manchester University Press.

Lilleker, D. G., & Negrine, R. (2006). Mapping a market orientation: Can we only detect political marketing through the lens of hindsight? In P. J. Davies & B. I. Newman (Eds.), *Winning elections with political marketing* (pp. 33-56). New York, Haworth Press.

Lilleker, D. G., & Scullion, R. (Eds.). (2008). *Voters or consumers: Imagining the contemporary electorate.* Newcastle: Cambridge Scholars Publishing.

Mandelson, P. (2002). *The Blair revolution revisited.* (New ed.). London: Politico's. (Original ed., 1996).

Marquand, D. (2004). *Decline of the public: The hollowing out of citizenship.* Oxford: Polity.

Miller, D., & Philo, G. (1999). The effective media. In G. Philo (Ed.), *Message received: Glasgow Media Group research, 1993-1998* (pp. 21-32). Harlow: Longman.

Moloney, K. (2006). *Rethinking public relations: PR propaganda and democracy.* (2nd ed.). London: Routledge. (Original ed., 2000)

Murdock, G., & Golding, P. (1989). Information poverty and political inequality: Citizenship in the age of privatized communications. *Journal of Communication, 39* (3), 180-95.

Negrine, R. (1994). *Politics and the mass media in Britain.* (2nd ed.). London: Routledge. (Original ed., 1989).

Norris, P. (2000). *A virtuous circle: Political communications in postindustrial societies.* Cambridge: Cambridge University Press.

Ornstein, N. J., & Mann, T. E. (Eds.). (2000). *The permanent campaign and its future.* Washington, DC: American Enterprise Institute; Brookings Institution.

O'Shaughnessy, N. J. 2002). The marketing of political marketing. In N. J. O'Shaughnessy (Ed.) & S. C. M.

Henneberg (Assoc. Ed.), *The idea of political marketing* (pp. 209-20). Westport, CT: Praeger.

Plato. (1977). *The republic* (D. Lee, Trans.). 2nd ed. Harmondsworth: Penguin. (Original ed. of this translation, 1955).

Rawnsley, G. D. (2004). *Political communication and democracy*. Basingstoke: Palgrave Macmillan.

Rosenbaum, M. (1997). *From soapbox to soundbite: Party political campaigning in Britain since 1945*. Basingstoke: Macmillan.

Rush, M. (2001). *The role of the Member of Parliament since 1868: From gentlemen to players*. Oxford: Oxford University Press.

Savigny, H. (2008). *The problem of political marketing*. New York: Continuum.

Scammell, M. (1995). *Designer politics: How elections are won*. Basingstoke: Macmillan.

Schumpeter, J. A. (1983). *The theory of economic development: An inquiry into profits, capital, credit, interest, and the business cycle* (R. Opie, Trans.). (New ed.). New Brunswick, NJ: Transaction Books. (Original work published, 1912).

Scullion, R. (2006). Investigating electoral choice through a 'consumer as choice-maker' lens. In D. G. Lilleker, N. A. Jackson & R. Scullion (Eds.), *The marketing of political parties: Political marketing at the 2005 British general election* (pp. 185-205). Manchester, Manchester University Press.

Scullion, R. (2008). The impact of the market on the character of citizenship, and the consequences of this for political engagement. In D. G. Lilleker & R. Scullion (Eds.), *Voters or consumers: Imagining the contemporary electorate* (pp. 51-72). Newcastle: Cambridge Scholars Publishing.

Slayden, D., & Whillock, R. K. (Eds.). (1999). *Soundbite culture: The death of discourse in a wired world.* Thousand Oaks, CA: Sage.

Temple, M. (2006). Dumbing down is good for you. *British Politics, 1* (1), 257-73.

Thomas, J. (2005). *Popular newspapers, the Labour Party and British politics.* London: Routledge.

Thompson, J. (2000). *Political scandal: Power and visibility in the media age.* Cambridge: Polity Press.

CHANGING REPRESENTATIONS OF RACE IN THE NEWS: THEORETICAL, EMPIRICAL, AND POLICY IMPLICATIONS

Ian Law

Introduction

The purpose of this chapter is to assess firstly, the methods and approaches that may be used to examine racism in news media output, and secondly, the extent to which representation of race, ethnic minorities and migrants has changed over the last twenty years. The International Federation of Journalists (2007) recently identified two conflicting roles that media professionals play in this context. On the one hand, they are often deemed responsible for shaping racism and intolerance, promoting ethnic, racial and religious hatred and inciting associated violence. On the other hand, they have contributed to the fight against racism, covering the struggle against apartheid and the Palestinian intifada, exposing racism, discrimination and human rights abuses and advocating for equality and justice. It is important to identify and address both these broad standpoints when investigating patterns of representation, as one might expect to find both these traits of journalism in UK news organisations. Moreover, which of these frames of reference dominates news coverage? How and why has change occurred? And what needs to be done by institutions and organisations in this field?

This chapter will address these questions, drawing on some key arguments presented in *Race in the News* (Law, 2002). I argued in the book that race has been a particularly newsworthy topic in Britain, Western Europe and the USA for over 250 years. Over this time, the news media have been a key site for the representation of ideas about racialised groups, providing a source of mass speculation, commentary and information. This cultural archive provides an immense store of knowledge, values and images, which have assisted in the maintenance and reproduction of both racist and anti-racist ideas, fusing in both historical and contemporary forms of racial ambivalence. Fascination with the allure of race and racism and their contradictions, degradations and pleasures seems to ensure that their representation in the media, and particularly treatment and coverage in news and factual programming, remains today a controversial and recurring issue of debate. In a recent, extensive US study of race and media, including news coverage, Entman and Rojecki confirm that "complex ambivalence" characterises White racial attitudes, and that various media, including television, film and advertising, play a "depleting role" by reducing social understanding. This, in turn, shifts prevailing ambivalence towards racial animosity (Entman & Rojecki, 2000, p. 44). Harmful "voids" or silences in the media, such as the pervasive nature of the ways in which White households benefit from the social division of welfare in terms of health care, social security and education, parallel the presentation of an irresponsible Black social world through stereotypes of laziness, welfare cheating, murderous violence and sexual excess. This chapter, and the research on which it draws, develops from a similar analytical concern, that of seeking to identify and address the ways in which the privileging and silencing of key themes operates in race news.

Back to fundamentals: Conceptualising media racism

The complex character of racism, which varies across cultural contexts and times, poses considerable problems for intellectual analysis. The process of conceptualisation involves constructing an adequate encompassing definition, identifying key common elements and their articulation and operationalising these elements to enable measurement and evaluation. Firstly, I consider the problem of conceptual definition and some of the difficulties of operationalisation (Law, 1996). The notion of racism as a singular, transhistorical phenomenon has often been challenged. Contemporary accounts deflate its explanatory power and develop historically and culturally grounded analysis, with particular attention being given to form and context. This is evident in Hall's (1992) emphasis on the "demise of the essential Black subject". Here, the construction of the universal commonalities of experiencing racism amongst all Black people in political mobilisation gives way to exploration of the huge variety of discrete ethnic identities which have emerged as a result of worldwide migrations (diasporas). The "stuff" of racism and who becomes its target varies widely within and across nation states. This has led to an emphasis on the specification and investigation of different racisms. But this strategy avoids the conceptual problem of definition of racism as based on a concept of race. Also, constructing a more robust transnational understanding of racism is particularly important in the context of increasing global communications (Ginneken, 1998). Therefore, the concept of racism can be distinguished by:

- the signification of race characteristics to identify a collectivity;

47

- the attribution of negative biological or cultural characteristics to such a group;

- the designation of boundaries to specify inclusion and exclusion;

- variation in form, in that it may be a relatively coherent theory or a loose assembly of images and explanations;

- its practical adequacy, in that it successfully "makes sense" of the world for those who articulate it (Miles, 1989, pp. 79-80);

- its pleasures: "an unearned easy feeling of superiority and the facile cementing of group identity on the fragile basis of arbitrary antipathy" (Shohat & Stam, 1994, p. 22).

Using the definition given above, racism involves the signification of race to define a collectivity and its linkage to negative attributes. Specification is therefore required of these two key elements: the signification of race and the evaluation of negative attribution. It is crucial to stress that races are entirely mythical and imagined creations.

Our first task is to identify exactly when and where race is being referred to in a text. For example, does the use of a photograph of a person's face in a news story carry a racial meaning? We might agree when, for example, a young, male, Black offender's mugshot is used to illustrate a story of gang rape. But also showing White people in particular roles, e.g. as experts in news stories, may equally hail particular White subjectivities and convey a racial meaning. So, when is race being signified and when is it not? Further, how are we to arbitrate in disputes over racial meaning? The concept of signification draws on the analysis of signs which has developed from the work of Saussure and Barthes: (see Hall [1997] for an introduction to these ideas). A sign is the association of the signifier (a picture, word or thing) with the signified (an idea, concept, mental picture or meaning). In this case the signified, race, refers to a distinct collectivity which is seen to share common physical characteristics. Signifiers of race may include words (e.g. Black, White, Caucasian, Negroid, ethnic, immigrant, Gypsy) or pictures (persons of common skin colour) and are open to complexity and variation in meaning and interpretation. The "normality" of constructions and representations of whiteness, combined with discursive strategies of racial denial, pose particular problems for media analysis (Gabriel, 1998). But the key point that the meaning of racial representations "can never be fixed" (Hall, 1997, p. 270) is illustrated by the varied and conflicting means employed to identify and measure such meaning.

Our second task is the measurement of the negative attribution of race. Negative attribution is often treated (Glasgow Media Group 1997a, 1997b) in a vague and ambiguous manner, and may have a range of meanings, depending on how this is assessed. These include:

- Whitecentrism: measurement of negative attribution of minorities against a dominant White norm;

- Mimetic accuracy: assessment of racial and cultural representation in comparison to "real" life;

- Eurocentrism: evaluation of the privileging and silencing of different cultural voices in relation to Eurocentric norms;

- Racialised voices: perception of negative attribution of racialised groups by themselves.

i) *Whitecentrism*

The comparison of treatment against a "White norm" is often used in the assessment of the portrayal of minority ethnic groups in television programmes. This may be a useful method for the construction of arguments around issues of inequity and unfairness in programmes and films; but this approach implies that portrayals of minority ethnic groups should conform with the pattern of portrayals of Whites, and therefore places "White" norms at the centre of the analysis and privileges these as given and unquestioned. In the UK, work by the Glasgow Media Group (1997a, 1997b; Philo, 1999) has sought to operationalise such a whitecentric analysis through the study of the proportional representation of ethnic minority individuals as presenters and hosts on British television and in television advertising. In the USA, Entman and Rojecki use this method to produce an index of media treatment of race (see http://www.raceandmedia.com). They provide comparison of Black and White roles in film, appearance in television advertisements and entertainment shows, and representation in news stories. They are careful to distance themselves from any argument that attempts to assess quantitative representation in relation to reality: e.g. where reporting of Black perpetrators of crime in local television and press news items may appear to be over-representation in comparison to crime statistics. However, they also seek to move beyond quantitative whitecentric analysis to unravel the discursive construction of American whiteness.

The interrogation of the significance and role of whiteness in media representations through a deeper analysis of meaning is a feature of more recent debates. Amongst others, the call to investigate whiteness and White supremacist stereotypes has been made by West (1990), Frankenberg (1993), Dyer (1997) and Gabriel (1998). Gabriel (1998, p. 187) refers to the "eruption of whiteness" resulting from processes of globalisation, and the reassertion of whiteness as a device for "maintaining traditions, representing cultures and anchoring identities" in the face of rapid economic and cultural change. Interestingly, the media is seen here as one of the pivotal mechanisms in challenging the historically stable centrality of White dominant norms. Hence, the media is cast as radically subversive in its powerful disruption of White cultural identity. Gabriel's work is particularly valuable in articulating both contemporary uses/forms of whiteness and corresponding strategies of resistance and intervention. He identifies White pride politics: the explicitly racist celebration of whiteness; normative whiteness: implicitly racialised political discourses, bound to liberal universalism, national identity and cultural forms (sport, music, film); lastly, progressive whiteness: a politics which condemns both White pride and normative whiteness and perpetuates "White" dominance, characterised in Greg Dyke's description of the BBC as "hideously white" ("Dyke: BBC", 2001, January 6). This analytical approach opens up valuable terrain for discursive interrogation of media representation, which moves well beyond the rather mechanistic strategies of assessing whitecentrism set out above.

ii) *Mimetic accuracy*

Secondly, evaluation of negative attribution and negative representation may be made in relation to the "real" through examination of mimetic, or imitative, accuracy. Shohat and Stam (1994) highlight the values and weaknesses of this approach. They emphasise the value of a "progressive realism", which can be used effectively to "unmask and combat hegemonic representations". The many examples of passionate protest over distorted representation, based on these claims for progressive realism, range from that of Pakistanis in Bradford over their portrayal as the emerging "Muslim underclass" in a sensationalist BBC Panorama documentary, *Underclass in Purdah* (Minhas, 1993), to wider criticism from Muslim groups over Islamophobia in the British media and to Native American criticism of complacent ignorance in their portrayal as Red Indians in Hollywood films (Aleiss, 2005). In questioning the effectiveness of this stereotypes-and-distortions approach, Shohat and Stam refer to the "obsession with realism", which assumes that the "real" and the "truth" about a community are easily accessible, unproblematic and pre-existing.

iii) *Eurocentrism*

Thirdly, following on from this critique, Shohat and Stam reject "naive referential verism" and instead favour an analysis which focuses upon the "orchestration of discourses and perspectives" based on a commitment to polycentric multiculturalism. This is seen as involving a move from analysing images to analysing "voice", where the critics' task is to pinpoint the "cultural voices at play and those drowned out". This involves a conceptual shift from the analysis of racism to an analysis of colonialist Eurocentrism, where the basis of assessment is how far

European social, economic and cultural norms are used negatively to attribute the norms of others.

iv) *Racialised voices*

Fourthly, assessment of negative attribution of race may be made through an analysis of the perceptions of the members of that signified race. Karen Ross (1997, p. 244) reports both the "aching desire for Black images to be created, reported, discussed and interpreted in ways which recognise their humanity, not simply their blackness" (Daniels, 1990) and the "unbearable scrutiny" to which Black audiences subject the few Black characters on television. The key distinction that Ross highlights is the gulf in knowledge between "White" media practitioners and "Black" audiences of the detail of everyday life in minority ethnic households and communities. This privileges the role of Black and minority ethnic groups as critics with a right to be heard. The problems of counterposing "races" is acknowledged by Ross, who is sensitive to both the homogenisation of blackness and the strategic need to retain and establish the commonalities in the perceptions of ethnic and "racial" groups.

Audience research by Mullan (1996) for the Independent Television Commission [ITC] showed that most White viewers felt that news and current affairs programmes were fair (71%), whereas 59% of African-Caribbeans and 37% of Asians saw these programmes as biased against them through perpetuation of stereotypes, lack of explanatory context and choice of issues for inclusion and exclusion. Minority ethnic perceptions of news content fitted closely with the definition of institutional racism used in the Stephen Lawrence Inquiry; these included perceptions of racial and ethnic bias against them, an inappropriate service for people from differing cultural and ethnic groups, and prejudice, ignorance, thoughtlessness and racist stereotyping which disadvantages minority ethnic people (Macpherson, 1999).

A range of competing approaches are therefore available for assessing representation of race in the news and central concern over institutional racism. These have been used by a range of scholars in assessing the complex relation, flagged above, between "the media" and race over more than two decades.

Representing race in the news in the late 1980s

Studies of the news across the UK, USA, Canada, Netherlands, Germany, France, Italy and Australia have all produced findings that show the complex ways in which ideas about "race" have been reproduced through reporting about minority ethnic groups and migration (Dijk, 1991; Jakubowicz, 1994; Campbell, 1995; Valdivia, 1995; Iyengar & Reeves, 1997; Meyers, 1997). A common finding is the confinement of coverage to a set of limited topics (Dijk, 1993):

- Immigration and associated debates over numbers, illegal entry, fraudulent activities, forms of confinement and control, and the threat to society, culture and nation;

- Crime, with special attention to racialised crime, such as mugging, rioting, drugs offences, prostitution and violent offences;

- Cultural difference, which is often inflated, negatively interpreted and linked to social problems, including inner city decline and unemployment;

- Ethnic relations, including inter-ethnic tension, violence and discrimination.

In addition, the silence on a range of topics of relevance to ethnic minorities is noted, along with the prominence given to White news actors and the marginalisation of minority representatives, while minority women and anti-racist voices have been subject to criticism. Analysis of selected sources from the British press in the 1980s showed that in only 4% of items on minority ethnic affairs were groups allowed to speak for themselves (Dijk, 1993, p. 254). Gordon and Rosenberg (1989) used selected examples, and Dijk (1991) a more exhaustive content and discourse analysis, to substantiate a comprehensive critique of racism in the British press in the 1980s. Comparing analysis of headline coverage in 1985/86 to 1989, Dijk (1991) notes that "ethnic reporting has become less negative and aggressive". Overall, coverage is seen as less blatantly racist than in the 1960s and 1970s, but that stereotypes and definitions of minorities as a "problem" and "threat" are still a persistent problem (Dijk, 1991, p. 245).

Representing race in the news in the 1990s

Overall, therefore, most studies of race in the news are highly selective and miss the "big picture" of the complete set of themes and range of stories presented. The benchmark empirical study presented in *Race in the News* (Law, 2002) aimed to address this gap in knowledge and called for an inquiry into institutional racism in news organisations. In the next few paragraph, I review the findings of the main study.

Daily coverage of race news on television, radio and in the broadsheet and tabloid press was analysed over a six month period between November 1996 and May 1997; this showed *a significant shift in coverage between the 1980s and the 1990s, from overt hostility to anti-racism towards the presentation of an "anti-racist show"*. It was argued that this "great anti-racist show" may, in some news organisations, be operating as an outward, empty attempt of display, masking continuing normative and progressive whiteness in news organisations, racial and ethnic inequalities of power and employment and a collective failure to provide appropriate quality news services for Black and minority ethnic communities and consumers. Such a "show" may well cover a backcloth of institutional racism. Nonetheless, in the case study of British news, about *three quarters of news items studied presented a broadly anti-racist message*, including items which sought to expose and criticise racist attitudes, statements, actions and policies, which addressed the concerns of immigrant and minority ethnic groups and showed their contribution to British society, and which embraced an inclusive view of multicultural British identity. Complex factors account for this process, including changing cultural, political and government discourse over race issues, changes in the minority ethnic employment profile in some news organisations, increasing recognition of anti-racism and multiculturalism in regulatory environments and competitive rivalry in news production. The balance between pro-minority and anti-minority messages varied across news media, with television news carrying the highest proportion of anti-racist messages (83%) and the tabloids carrying the smallest proportion (66%). The largest thematic category of race news contained stories relating to crime and violence, with little proportional thematic difference across television, radio and the tabloids. In addition, immigration was more likely to be treated in a sympathetic and humanitarian fashion, the press silence on Black people as victims of violence was found no longer to exist, multiculturalism and Islam were more likely to be valued than vilified in news items and there was little coverage seeking to deny the existence of racism. Also, there was a pattern of decline in the quantity of race-related press items since the mid-1980s, despite the coverage of the Stephen Lawrence Inquiry. This may indicate a lessening of the "race relations" frame in British news coverage and a reduction in the coverage of minority ethnic affairs and migration. The "fit" between race news selected by editors and the real pattern of race-related newsworthy events is, as with other types of news, likely to be poor (Gunter, 1997).

The growing strength of broadly anti-racist news values goes hand in hand with a significant core group of news messages that foster racism, animosity and hatred. In Britain, about *a quarter of news items conveyed a negative message about minority groups. The daily repetition of linkages between race, violence, dangerousness and crime is a constant feature of news* in general. Also, key "old" news frames, or traditional racist messages, persist; for instance, the presentation of selective groups of citizens and migrants as a welfare burden who are prone to deception, fraud and other forms of crime. Hence, racialised forms of social control are justified, including race-driven forms of policing and discriminatory forms of immigration control. By these means, Black, Asian and other migrant groups are constructed as a social problem in a range of ways, often with little attention to real social welfare issues amongst those communities, such as homelessness, poor housing, poor educational opportunities and restricted provision of health services and social welfare.

Reporting on migration issues was found to be a continuing source of racial hostility. This has been often fuelled by government sources by means of concern expressed over abuse, fraud and deceit and other forms of illegal activity. News coverage of this issue has been shown to be often characterised by sloppy journalism, with little attention to the real costs and benefits of complex migration flows. The news media, particularly the press, selectively repeat, rework and re-invent a simple pattern of key racist messages which have "helped to build a respectable, coherent, common-sense whiteness" (Gabriel 1998, p. 188). In addition, the crucial "steering" role of the major political parties, and in particular government leadership on these issues, was established as central to the rise and fall of media hostility to racialised migrant groups.

Overall, however, the assessment of bias in news reporting was found to be a complex affair involving a range of strategies to evaluate news presentation, selection, balance and impartiality (Gunter, 1997). Editorial bias in selection of race items was indicated by the identification of differing news agendas across different news media. An *evaluation of more deliberate racial bias in British news content confirmed the evidence of significant progress and improvement in reporting race issues in the news media in comparison to the 1980s.* Overall, most items were found to be neutral, with more evidence that journalists were prepared to advocate on behalf of minorities than express deliberate hostility towards them. In Northern Ireland, however, a study of newspapers showed that these encouraging trends were not in evidence (Hainsworth, 1998). Minority ethnic groups' concerns were largely marginalised in the news, reflecting weak political leadership, poor journalistic professionalism and unconscious racism.

Judging by the available evidence, therefore, a "great anti-racist show" is live and kicking in British news, and, as with many forms of entertainment, tried and tested formulas prevail. Anti-racist rhetoric is strong and exposing the stupidity of racism does make front-page news. Here, there is a recurring tendency to refer to the racist comments of public figures as "gaffes". Ingrained racism is thus reduced to the status of an unconscious indiscreet blunder. News organisations and journalists seem to be working within established discursive conventions of what anti-racism should be about, as opposed to elevating the "unexpected" and pushing forward the serious debate over how to shift British racism fundamentally. Further, it is such "unwitting stereotyping" that was shown to be the driving force for systematic institutional racism by the Lawrence Inquiry. Nevertheless, it is better to see racism ridiculed in the news than anti-racism. There was a virtual silence about the "stupidity" and "lunacy" of anti-racism policies and initiatives in the late 1990s. The dominant news frame in the 1980s has gone and this does indicate the extent to which anti-racist discourse has permeated news organisations and may now be a more "normal" news value itself. As yet, a further shift in race news forwards (or backwards) to an increasing focus on the problems of White individuals and groups "spoken through the language of racism" (Mac an Ghaill, 1999) has not taken place. The plight of White victims of racism has been highlighted in news stories, but these remain infrequent in comparison to the volume of coverage dealing with minority ethnic victims of racism.

Of course, this pattern may quickly change, with new angles and images used to move beyond conventional approaches to race issues in news reporting, particularly given the volatile, ambivalent and fickle character of this "anti-racist show". A simple retreat from this position also seems to occur regularly in some sections of some news media: e.g. the *Daily Mail*, where it has become fashionable again to pour vitriol on attempts to challenge racism and where backward-looking forms of cultural affirmation are used to provide strong, entirely "sensible" justifications for advocating racial and cultural purity and hostility to those outside the White nation. On the other hand, the Stephen Lawrence story dominated the news during this study and was described as the *"biggest sea change in media coverage of race"*, by Michael Mansfield QC in the *Guardian* on the 19th April, 1999. He notes the indifference of news organisations and current affairs programmes to the case early on (1993/94) compared to the extensive news, documentary and drama coverage more recently. Also, in relation to race crime more generally, there were significant improvements in both local and national coverage. What this sea change will bring next in terms of trends in race news is uncertain and unknown. At best, we can expect courage, innovation and creativity in identifying institutional racism and forms of racial, ethnic and cultural exclusion. In Britain, the overall picture of institutional racism that emerged from news coverage highlighted the immigration service, criminal justice organisations, football clubs, health authorities and trusts, the armed forces and private employers like Fords as key problem sectors. There is no silence here about the range and diversity of institutional racism and racism is not simply reduced to the problem of racist individuals, as some critics have suggested (Gordon & Rosenberg, 1989). The improved news coverage of anti-racist campaigning activity is a key change since the 1980s, one which reflects increased openness to minority voices. British news and documentary making contains a powerful thread of output that excels in carrying these messages and debates forward. The renewal of confidence in anti-racist voices, together with strong anti-racist political leadership, may further strengthen and deepen this process across the news media. *In America, the development of an "anti-racist show" in news content does seem to be a weaker trend than in the UK.* Recent research highlights the dominance of ongoing problems in the portrayal of Blacks and Whites and little in the way of effective anti-racist journalism (Entman & Rojecki, 2000).

However, evidence (Law, 2002, chap. 4) indicates the changing shape and style of anti-racism in US news, in which political leadership is again a key factor. There were strong parallels in political positions taken by parties and leaders in the 1997 UK general election and in the 2000 US full-term elections. Talking-up ethnic diversity and the significance of the non-White vote and keeping silent on issues of immigration were marked features of this cross-party consensus. In the UK, the fragility of this consensus has been shown in recent political and social conflict over recent waves of migration; this is also a likely scenario in the USA. Nevertheless, partly because of the impact of these strategies, there has been significant progress in minority representation in media organisations in the USA, as employment in newspapers increased from 4% to 11% between 1978 and 1998. The figure, particularly with respect to newspapers, is much lower in Britain, owing to much feebler investment and effort in positive action strategies which seek to shift White dominance in employment. Overall, there has been a *general lack of attention to the under-representation of minority ethnic groups in the British news media.* In the absence of adequate representation of minority ethnic groups in major news organisations, particularly at a senior level, audiences from those groups will probably continue to remain concerned about bias in the production of news and dissatisfied with the quality and appropriateness of news services. *The persistence of a significant core of hostile racist news messages and the failure of legal and regulatory action to provide an effective response to these problems warrants more comprehensive action.* While many social institutions in the UK, including the armed forces, have been subject to thorough investigation of institutional racism, news organisations have not.

Technological and regulatory changes are increasingly producing an environment that facilitates rapid changes in news organisations and their output. Media industry fragmentation, flexible working practices and changing relationships between news producers and their multicultural audiences are producing great opportunities for improving the provision of appropriate and professional news services. In this context, it is realistic to place on major news organisations a burden of expectation that coverage should continue to show a trend of improvement. This would mean:

- extending the news coverage of various forms of racism, racial violence, racial discrimination, persistent forms of White privilege and initiatives to tackle racism and promote ethnic equality and cultural diversity;

- producing more news that highlights the contribution of minority ethnic groups and migrant groups to British society, not just individuals in entertainment and sport;

- providing more informed news coverage about migration, which promotes better understanding of the benefits and complexities of migrant flows;

- promoting debate and public understanding about the ethnic and cultural diversity of people living in Britain and abroad;

- eradicating the deliberate shaping of news items that show, present or promote hostility to minority ethnic groups;

- increasing precision, accuracy and attention to relevance and social identity in identifying the ethnic origin of groups and individuals;

- developing an extended range of initiatives and innovations to improve ethnic minority representation in news organisations;

- ensuring explicit attention to issues of anti-racism and ethnic diversity in legislative, regulatory and policy environments in which news organisations operate;

- abandoning old/traditional race relations and immigration frames in presenting news events and finding new ways to present issues of social diversity, division and difference;

- tackling institutional racism in news organisations in specific relation to the provision of news services to all groups and audiences.

A new context of declining media, political and social hostility to both settled minority ethnic groups and new migrant groups can provide the conditions for the creation of a climate of greater trust, in which more open discussion and debate of sensitive issues affecting minority ethnic groups in the news can fruitfully take place.

These more progressive social spaces are continually subject to the swift remembering, reinvention and restatement of hostile messages, as seen in the UK in the first years of this century, with increasing vilification of asylum seekers and refugees.

Representing race in the news in the 21st century

In January 2006, it was highly unexpected to see a new call for the news media to tackle institutional racism coming from Sir Ian Blair, the Metropolitan Police Commissioner. This echoed the author's call for such an investigation based on evidence from a decade earlier. The Commissioner attacked newspapers for their differential racialised treatment of murder victims and compared their treatment with that of the police: "we do devote the same level of resources to murders in relation to their difficulty, the difference is how they are reported. I actually believe the media is guilty of institutional racism in the way they report deaths" (Gibson & Dodd, 2006). Newspaper editors were very quick to dismiss his claims and Trevor Phillips from the Commission for Racial Equality [CRE] argued that "a blanket condemnation of the media belongs to yesterday and not today. The media could still do more to be even-handed in its reporting" (Gibson & Dodd). However, it is interesting to note that only a few months later, the CRE published two reports that did just that. *Careers in print media: What people from ethnic minorities think* (MORI, 2006), and *Why ethnic minority workers leave London's print journalism sector* (Thanki & McKay, 2006) both identified the racialisation of news organisations. The second report showed that workplace norms in print journalism were shot through with everyday racism in terms of attitudes, language and treatment of ethnic minority journalists. The first CRE report showed that ethnic minorities were aware and conscious of high levels of racism and discrimination in this sector.

Furthermore, there is no doubting the fundamental

shift and focus in representation of race in the news that has taken place in the last five to ten years, with an obsessive focus on and debate surrounding Muslim issues. This was clearly shown to have been occurring prior to 9/11 by Richardson in *Mis-representing Islam* (2004). His research found that broadsheet newspapers argued predominantly that Muslims are homogenous, separate, inferior, the enemy; newspapers could be regarded as Islamophobic, predominantly reframing Muslim cultural difference as cultural deviance and increasingly as a cultural threat, whether a military or terrorist threat, a threat to the democratic stability of other countries or a threat to women. Underlying this is a central dominant idea that Muslims are essentially barbarians in need of civilisation. Richardson's analysis identified a set of key frames of meaning, prior to 9/11, available for journalists to draw on in interpreting more recent events.

Lastly, new research on the role of the local press shows a highly uneven picture. A comprehensive review of West Yorkshire press coverage of race reporting during the 2005 General Election (Law, Basi, & Farrar, 2006) concluded that more than three quarters of the stories were either unbiased or displayed a positive stance towards ethnic minorities. More than 400 race-related items appeared in the *Keighley News, Bradford Telegraph & Argus, Yorkshire Post* and *Yorkshire Evening Post* in April and May 2005. "Race" featured mainly in General Election stories, crime reports and in items about community engagement. Only 10% of news items related to the British National Party [BNP] and most of these showed it in a negative light. The BNP received unfavourable coverage in 37 articles, while 23 items reported the party in neutral terms. Prominence was given in the *Yorkshire Evening Post* to the late Robin Cook's exhortation to vote against BNP candidates wherever they stood. The only items supportive of the BNP were letters to the editor of the *Keighley News*. Most negative stories about ethnic minorities (35 items) regarded allegations of election fraud within the Asian community. In the crime stories, ethnic minorities appeared as victims of crime alongside cases where the perpetrator was Black or Asian. Of community engagement stories, almost a third were supportive of ethnic minorities and the rest were neutral. Only 12% of stories were about asylum seekers, of which half were negative. The *Yorkshire Post* printed the most negative articles on asylum seekers (a total of 15 items), while the *Yorkshire Evening Post* contained no negative stories and eight positive items on asylum seekers.

The report co-author, Max Farrar said: "Our findings are, overall, very encouraging. It seems that the Yorkshire journalists have taken to heart the criticisms that have been made of earlier coverage of race issues and have gone a long way towards cleaning up their act. I hope they keep this up during the future elections." Tina Basi, the third author, said: "Given the current climate surrounding the debate on the freedom of speech, research examining the media and representations of race and ethnicity has become increasingly significant, both for the academic community and journalists. Despite the negative coverage of asylum seekers, there were several positive stories on race, particularly focusing on community engagement, multiculturalism, and women as key voters in the Asian community." In commenting on the findings of the report, *Bradford Telegraph & Argus* editor Perry Austin-Clarke said:

I'm very pleased to see that the *T & A* receives such a positive assessment in this research. We pride ourselves on our reputation for, and record of, unbiased and constructive reporting of race and community issues, which has been recognised three times in recent years with national Race in the Media awards from the Commission for Racial Equality. We believe in reporting Bradford and district as a single community: we don't sectionalise coverage or stereotype our ethnic minority reporters to cover only ethnic or race affairs. We expect every reporter to get to know all sections of our community and to treat every member of the public, whatever their background, fairly and equally. At the same time, we believe it is important not to fight shy of the genuine concerns of some parts of the community and to help stimulate open and objective debate. We take pride in reporting the positive developments in community relations and we have taken a deliberate stance against the BNP, whose underlying views we believe to be abhorrent despite their thin veneer of respectability. We're not perfect, of course, but we believe we are making a positive contribution to the future of community relations in Bradford and district and we hope to continue to do so. (Personal communication, by email)

Patterns of improving coverage of race, ethnicity and migration in the British press were further supported by this study. We need to recognise the positive contribution local press can play in improving community relations and the understanding of ethnic diversity. In relation to local press coverage of asylum seekers, persistent themes of reducing migrant rights, the burden on the welfare state and the dishonesty of migrants have been regularly presented with active shaping of editorial hostility. A 2004 study by the Information Centre about Asylum and Refugees in the UK [ICAR] showed how this directly contributes to increased community tension and harassment of asylum seekers, but it did also show how the local press were more positive in some areas. This is confirmed by Finney's (2004) work on press portrayals of asylum seeker dispersal. She shows how the *South Wales Echo* took a very different perspective to national discourse and examines how positive and humanitarian-focused coverage contested and challenged negative portrayals.

Conclusion

To conclude, racism and anti-racism are powerful twin social forces that will continue to shape news communications and news organisations through the twenty-first century. They operate in many different ways across national and international contexts, and much work is still to be done to map this complicated terrain. A good example is Lokshina's recent study (2006) of hate speech in Russia, which draws on monitoring analysis of a range of national and regional newspapers and some websites, thus providing a systematic overview. This piece is rare in identifying the big picture of media messages and highlights the positive tendencies in media communications that need to be considered alongside expressions of hostility and superiority. We continually need to be alert to this global context of racial ambivalence.

This chapter has identified the need to sharpen the conceptual tools that are used in analysing the representation of race, in terms of both conceptualising race and racism and in constructing frameworks for the evaluation of negative attribution. These frameworks involve the measurement of the negative attribution of minorities in relation to whiteness, assessment of racial and cultural representation in comparison to "real" life, evaluation of the privileging and silencing of different cultural voices in relation to Eurocentric norms, and privileging the perceptions of negative attribution held by racialised groups themselves.

The unevenly improving coverage of race news was established in an examination of coverage in the UK. In the context of the development of global approaches to tackling racist violence and conflict, this is acknowledged as a vital component of anti-racist strategy, as UNESCO has confirmed,

> The mass media and those who control or serve them, as well as all organized groups within national communities, are urged – with due regard to the principles embodied in the Universal Declaration of Human Rights, particularly the principle of freedom of expression – to promote understanding, tolerance and friendship among individuals and groups and to contribute to the eradication of racism, racial discrimination and racial prejudice, in particular by refraining from presenting a stereotyped, partial, unilateral or tendentious picture of individuals and of various human groups. Communication between racial and ethnic groups must be a reciprocal process, enabling them to express themselves and to be fully heard without let or hindrance. The mass media should therefore be freely receptive to ideas of individuals and groups which facilitate such communication. (1978, article 5, para. 3).

UNESCO's classic liberal model of anti-racism is fraught with dilemmas and difficulties (Law, 1996), with much more detailed consideration needed of the ownership and control of news media and the impact of new information and communication technologies. Nevertheless, in pursuing this UNESCO objective, the role of research by academics and non-governmental organisations [NGOs] is central in establishing the ways in which active shaping of both racist hostility and racial justice operates in news media output. Using such research to challenge patterns of

---

Cont_xts

representation is also vital, and Gabriel (1998) has examined a number of campaigns and groups who have sought to do this. The "call to arms" we have here is to carry through a fundamental challenge to institutional racism in news media organisations and for "engaged" academic work to assist in this task.

References

Aleiss, A. (2005). *Making the White man's Indian: Native Americans and Hollywood movies.* Westport, CT: Praeger.

Campbell, C. P. (1995). *Race, myth and the news.* London: Sage.

Daniels, T. (1990). Beyond negative and positive images. In J. Willis & T. Wollen (Eds.), *The neglected audience* (pp. 66-71). London: BFI Publishing.

Dijk, T. A. van (1991). *Racism and the press.* London: Routledge.

Dijk, T. A. van (1993). *Elite discourse and racism.* Newbury Park, CA: Sage.

Dyer, R. (1997). *White.* London: Routledge.

Dyke: BBC is 'hideously white'. (2001, January 6). *BBC News.* Retrieved September 11, 2008, from: http://news.bbc.co.uk/1/hi/scotland/1104305.stm

Entman, R. M., & Rojecki, A. (2000). *The Black image in the White mind: Media and race in America.* Chicago: University of Chicago Press.

70

Finney, N. (2004). *Asylum seeker dispersal: Public attitudes and press portrayals around the U.K.* Unpublished doctoral dissertation, University of Wales, Swansea.

Frankenberg, R. (1993). *White women, race matters: The social construction of whiteness.* London: Routledge.

Gabriel, J. (1998). *Whitewash: Racialized politics and the media.* London: Routledge.

Gibson, O., & Dodd, V. (2006, January 27). Met chief labels media institutionally racist: Coverage of recent killings "points up divide": Allegations rejected by some editors. *The Guardian,* p. 7.

Ginneken, J. van, (1998*). Understanding global news: A critical introduction.* London: Sage.

Glasgow Media Group (1997a). *'Race' and the public face of television.* Glasgow: Author.

Glasgow Media Group (1997b). *Ethnic minorities in television advertising.* Glasgow: Author.

Gordon, P., & Rosenberg, D. (1989). *Daily racism: The press and Black people in Britain.* London : Runnymede Trust.

Gunter, B. (1997) *Measuring bias on television.* Luton: University of Luton Press.

Hainsworth, P. (Ed.). (1998). *Divided society: Ethnic minorities and racism in Northern Ireland*. London: Pluto Press.

Hall, S. (1992). The question of cultural identity. In S. Hall, D. Held & T. McGrew (Eds.), *Modernity and its futures* (pp. 274-316). Cambridge: Polity Press, in association with the Open University.

Hall, S. (Ed.). (1997). *Representation: Cultural representations and signifying practices*. London: Sage, in association with the Open University.

International Federation of Journalists. (2007). *Ethical journalism answer to race hate and war of words between cultures says IFJ congress*: [press release]. Retrieved September 12, 2008, from:
http://www.ifj.org/en/articles/ethical-journalism-answer-to-race-hate-and-war-of-words-between-cultures-says-ifj-congress-

Information Centre about Asylum and Refugees in the UK. (2004). *Media image, community impact: Assessing the impact of media and political images of refugees and asylum seekers on community relations in London: Report of a pilot research study, commissioned by the Mayor of London*. London: Author.

Iyengar, S., & Reeves, R. (Eds.). (1997). *Do the media govern?: Politicians, voters, and reporters in America.* London: Sage.

Jakubowicz, A. (Ed.). (1994). *Racism, ethnicity, and the media.* St Leonards, NSW: Allen & Unwin.

Law, I. (1996). *Racism, ethnicity, and social policy.* London: Prentice Hall.

Law, I. (2002). *Race in the news.* Basingstoke: Palgrave

Law, I., Basi, T. & Farrar, M. (2006). *Race in the local news.* Leeds: CERS

Lokshina, T. (2006). 'Hate speech' in the media: Monitoring prejudice in Russia. In J. H. Brinks, S. Rock, & E. Timms (Eds.), *Nationalist myths and modern media: Contested identities in the age of globalization* (pp. 201-214). London: I. B. Tauris.

Mac an Ghaill, M. (1999). *Contemporary racisms and ethnicities: Social and cultural transformations.* Buckingham: Open University Press.

Macpherson, W. (1999). *The Stephen Lawrence Inquiry: Report of an inquiry by Sir William Macpherson of Cluny.* London: Stationery Office.

Mansfield, M. (1999, April 19). Put race before ratings. *The Guardian*, p. 10.

Meyers, M. (1997). *News coverage of violence against women: Engendering blame.* Thousand Oaks, CA: Sage.

Miles, R. (1989). *Racism.* London: Routledge.

Minhas, N. (Producer). (1993, March 29). *Underclass in purdah* [Television broadcast]. London: British Broadcasting Corporation.

MORI (2006). *Careers in print media: What people from ethnic minorities think: A survey conducted by MORI for the Commission for Racial Equality.* London: Commission for Racial Equality.

Mullan, B. (1996). *Not a pretty picture: Ethnic minority views of television.* Aldershot: Avebury.

Philo, G. (Ed.). (1999). *Message received: Glasgow Media Group research, 1993-1998.* Harlow: Longman.

Richardson, J. E. (2004). *(Mis)representing Islam: The racism and rhetoric of British broadsheet newspapers.* Amsterdam: John Benjamins.

Ross, K. (1997). Viewing (p)leasure, viewer pain: Black audiences and British television. *Leisure Studies, 16,* 233-248.

Shohat, E., & Stam, R. (1994). *Unthinking Eurocentrism: Multiculturalism and the media.* London: Routledge.

Changing Representations of Race in the News

Thanki, A., & McKay, S. (2006). *Why ethnic minority workers leave London's print journalism sector: Final report for the Commission for Racial Equality, November 2005.* London: Commission for Racial Equality.

UNESCO. (1978). *Declaration on race and racial prejudice, adopted by the General Conference at its twentieth session, Paris, 27 November 1978* [Electronic version]. Retrieved July 31, 2007, from:

http://www.unesco.org/education/pdf/RACE_E.PDF

Valdivia, A. N. (Ed.). (1995). *Feminism, multiculturalism, and the media: Global diversities.* Thousand Oaks, CA: Sage.

West, C. (1990). The new cultural politics of difference. In R. Ferguson, M. Geever, T. T. Minh-ha & C. West (Eds.), *Out there: Marginalization and contemporary cultures* (pp. 19-36). New York: New Museum of Contemporary Art; Cambridge, MA: MIT Press.

CONSTRUCTING THE VICTIM AND PERPETRATOR OF DOMESTIC VIOLENCE

Paula Wilcox

Introduction

How we talk about domestic violence is very important; what is expressed and not expressed, the exchange of cultural attitudes, stories, jokes, all contribute to how individuals, communities and governments respond to domestic violence, as well as to the self-perception of domestic violence survivors and perpetrators. Public policy, and to some extent attitudes, on domestic violence have been shifting in the UK in recent years; what was once largely accepted behaviour is less tolerated today and indeed is recognised in law as a crime. Nevertheless, many myths about domestic violence remain and the media is a primary cultural site perpetuating such myths.

To date in the UK, there has been little if any academic investigation of the popular social construction of domestic violence; this paper therefore reviews existing literature on print media constructions of domestic violence, mainly from North America, as a precursor to carrying out empirical research on the topic. It looks at the print media's role in shaping stories, understandings and responses to this serious social problem and how the media constructs the female victim and the male perpetrator; as Gallagher argues, "It is in the comparison of how women and men are portrayed in the media that insights emerge, and change can ensue" (2004, p. 157).

The ways in which we talk about domestic violence are dependent upon how it is defined and what we know about it. Domestic violence is a highly complex and multifaceted concept involving a pattern of coercive behaviours in intimate partnerships[1], with the aim of one partner gaining control over the other partner. Such behaviours can range from verbal abuse/threats and coercion, to manipulation, physical and sexual violence, rape and homicide. At the level of the individual, therefore, experiencing domestic violence entails a major interpersonal struggle invoking honour, pride and shame (Wilcox, 2007). Such individual struggles are set in a context of very real social structures and long-term social processes which also shape the experience of domestic violence. Because domestic violence resists easy definition, it is difficult to gain accurate statistical data on its incidence and prevalence. We cannot be certain about the numbers of people it affects since it is a crime which frequently goes unrecorded.

However, what we do know from quantitative research and statistics and qualitative empirical research is that domestic violence in heterosexual partnerships is gender-specific and occurs far more frequently than official statistics reveal. Research consistently reveals that domestic violence in heterosexual relationships is most commonly perpetrated by men against women (Stanko, 2001; Walby & Allen, 2004; Home Office, 2005). We also know that domestic violence is part of a broader variety of violence which the United Nations terms "gender-based violence", a worldwide issue. The World Health Organization's first world report on violence and health (October 2002) found that violence against women accounts for approximately 7% of all deaths of women

---

[1] Domestic violence can also be defined as including family-type relationships, and also occurs in same-sex relationships, but in this paper I focus solely on intimate partner violence in heterosexual relationships.

aged 15-44; in some countries, up to 69% of women report having been physically assaulted. In Britain, according to recent figures from the British Crime Survey, about a quarter (26%) of women have been physically assaulted since the age of 16, while 6% have been assaulted in the previous year (Walby & Allen, 2004; Home Office, 2005). Whilst some men *are* subjected to domestic violence, the scale of male victimisation is considerably lower than that of females. Moreover, a high proportion of domestic violence perpetrators against men are also male. So, despite the problematic nature of statistical data on domestic violence, it affects the lives of many women and children. Indeed, since the mid-1990s it has been recognised by the United Nations (1995), in the Beijing Declaration and Platform of Action, as a violation of human rights. Is this how our print media conceptualises domestic violence? The paper examines how crime in general is constructed in print media, before turning to focus specifically on the construction of domestic violence.

The social construction of crime in print media

Social problems provide a key source of media stories; the media is thought to shape and transform social problems into stories with the aim of selling as many copies of the publication concerned as possible. Crime reporting is, in fact, more prevalent now and violent and sexual crimes are over-reported (Naylor, 2001; Greer, 2003). To sell copy, the media is prone to manipulate public perceptions, creating a false view of crime. As Jewkes (2004) points out, this can be achieved in different ways; for instance, through the use of stereotypes, bias, prejudice and even gross over-simplification of crime contexts. Often what people believe and think about a social problem has been largely constructed through claim-making in the media (Spector &

Kitsuse, 1987).

Crime stories in the media are significant because discourses on crime tell us about a culture's social, political and moral order. When newspapers report on a case of domestic violence, for example, this often initiates wider public discourse on how this event relates to broader questions about the moral health of the family. A conception of news as both constructed and productive of future discourse is, therefore, critical when examining news reports on domestic violence.

The embedded nature of news values and news selection processes are frequently held responsible for the patterns of news coverage. A number of themes identified in this paper reveal that this is the case: the under-representation of domestic violence; the over-representation of physical and extreme cases of domestic violence; the focus on victims as compared to the neglect of perpetrators of domestic violence; and the absence of a gendered analysis. Print media almost unfailingly portrays domestic violence (as well as other issues) as an individual problem, and what is more a problem for victims. As we shall see, there is scant attention paid to perpetrators of domestic violence in the limited coverage of domestic violence in print media.

The under-representation of domestic violence

The media is often criticised for paying too much attention to particular types of crime, particularly those of a violent and sexual nature which occur in the public sphere. When it comes to domestic violence[2], however, which mostly occurs in the home or private sphere, the opposite is the

---

[2] The same problem applies to coverage of child abuse by known others, as well as to white collar crime.

case. With regard to domestic violence, there is too little media interest rather than too much, especially in relation to the high prevalence and incidence of this crime. In the case of domestic violence, as Garside (2003) pointed out, reality can be as much distorted through under-reporting as through over-reporting. But what are the reasons for this paucity of reporting on domestic violence?

The masculinist lens through which domestic violence has been, and to some extent is still, perceived is one reason why there tends to be less press coverage than might be expected. Traditionally, violent assault has been defined as a coercive, aggressive act committed in the street, in a pub or any other public venue, which has largely involved male-on-male violence. Domestic violence, which largely takes place in the home, was not (and to some degree is still not) seen as a form of assault, despite the fact that it is the most likely form of assault to be suffered by a woman (Naffine, 1996, p. 65). Public assault (which a man is most likely to experience) then is the standard case, whereas domestic violence is viewed as "a special class of victimization … the complication" to the norm (Naffine, p. 65).

Furthermore, despite growing awareness of domestic violence as a social problem, it still remains largely hidden, owing to the social stigma attached to a woman admitting that she is experiencing it, while many people are likely to be unwilling to want to discuss this problem. That stigma and taboo attaches to both victims and perpetrators may in turn explain why media coverage, when it occurs, tends to cover only exceptional cases (as will be discussed later). In all countries where large-scale surveys have been conducted, the findings reveal that at least one in five women have been physically or sexually abused by an intimate partner at some time in their lives (World Health Organization, 2000). So, ironically perhaps, another explanation for the lack of coverage is that domestic violence may be perceived as too commonplace an occurrence to warrant news or media coverage and only rarely, in exceptional circumstances, is seen as newsworthy (Meyers, 1994, 1997).

But what impact does the under-representation of domestic violence have? Broadly, the implication is that the public largely continues to see domestic violence as someone else's problem, as well as being relatively rare. The under-reporting of domestic violence becomes part of the circle of dominant discourse which perpetuates the silencing and stigmatisation of this issue. It also impacts on domestic violence victims in that victims may decide that what they are experiencing cannot really be domestic violence, after all. And even when they do recognise themselves as victims, they are more likely to blame themselves as individuals rather than see domestic violence as a cultural and social problem to do with gendered power relationships.

In developed countries, knowledge about domestic violence is paradoxical, as on the one hand public awareness *has* increased dramatically, while on the other hand individuals tend to keep such knowledge at arm's length from their own situation (Pain, 1999), partly because of media gaps and silences and partly because of the emphasis in public discourse on "stranger danger". This means that if a woman does experience domestic violence from a partner or ex-partner, it comes as huge shock, rocking personal feelings of physical security as well as her hopes and aspirations about her marriage or partnership. This is so unexpected; it only happens to others; this can't be happening; what am I doing wrong?

The over-representation of physical and extreme cases of domestic violence

During 2001/02, 116 women were killed by a current or former male partner in England and Wales, an average of more than two women each week (Flood-Page & Taylor, 2003). As Boyle (2005) points out, media coverage of domestic violence follows Surette's (1998) "law of opposites", in that the stories reported tend to be domestic murders or the most unusual cases, as opposed to the most common stories. Murder of a wife/partner is clearly the most serious outcome of domestic violence and this potential must always be borne in mind. However, the news focus obscures the routine nature of domestic violence as mainly non-physical, psychological and emotional abuse, with physical and sexual violence(s) being employed far less frequently.

Emphasis on women's physical injuries as a result of domestic violence is not solely because of media sensationalism, however. It has also been an outcome of the predominant ways in which domestic violence comes into public view through victims' contacts with social agencies. Firstly, the *physical* injuries women sustain in domestic violence are extremely serious and can be life-threatening. Secondly, *physical* injuries are more likely to bring victims into contact with refuges/shelters, criminal justice and other social agencies. Thirdly, in our visual culture, demonstrating the *physical* injuries sustained by women is more straightforward and visually shocking than demonstrating other forms of injury[3]. However, the

---

[3] The "battered woman" is linked in the public imagination with visible injuries, and women experiencing domestic violence where there are no visible injuries may not see themselves as experiencing domestic violence.

media's emphasis on extreme cases of physical violence again distorts the reality of domestic violence. It has led to the widespread perception of domestic violence as separate and distinct *incidents* of *physical* violence rather than as an ongoing process of abuse, where the enactment of male power and control does not rely on violent acts alone. The focus on physical violence hence detracts from the seriousness of emotional abuses. However, feminist researchers have shown that women experience *emotional* abuse as a "deeper and more central form of abuse" (Kirkwood, 1993, p. 44). Moreover, women are far more likely to conceptualize *verbal* abuse as an expression of violence (Burman, Brown & Batchelor, 2003). The dominant understanding of domestic violence as *physical violence* hides the reality of the cumulative impact over time on women and children of what may seem from the outside to be relatively "minor" infringements of women's emotional and physical integrity; subtle acts can be very threatening:

> ... and when it come to birthdays and things like that he used to fall out wi' me so he didn't have to buy me anything, or owt like that, until he felt as though, you know, he knew he was going to lose me again, so he bought me an orchid. I don't know why he thought, I hated orchids! I hate orchids! [*laughs*] I hate orchids! He once bought me an eternity ring and, erm, it was second [hand], it were only twelve pounds, but it were something special, you know, I thought he was actually being nice, you know. And then as soon as he'd bought it he went, "and don't ask for anything else because you're not getting it", you know, I thought, oh God, you've spoilt it again. (Sally, as cited by Wilcox, 2006)

This commonplace aspect of ongoing "low-level" patterns of domestic abuse over time, sometimes interspersed with physical violence, is rarely if at all represented in print media stories on domestic violence.

The focus on victims and the neglect of perpetrators of domestic violence

The overwhelming finding from research on print media coverage of domestic violence is that the vast majority of stories focus on individual female victims, thereby continuing to construct the *public* issue of domestic violence as a private problem of women (Berns, 1999, 2001, 2004; Evans, 2001; Wykes, 2001; Boyle, 2005). This dominant individualistic perspective places responsibility on to female victims and normalises the idea that they should be held responsible for solving the problem of domestic violence.

Berns, who has researched the coverage of domestic violence in women's magazines in North America, points out that to write successfully on a social problem the story must "empower the victims, be primarily about one person, and have an upbeat and inspiring ending" (2004, p. 83). She suggests that the media does this in the following ways:

- With sympathetic and empowering perspectives that look at how women can take care of themselves;

- By informing readers about resources or services on how to solve the problem, prevent abuse or spot the signs of abuse;

- By keeping the story personal rather than looking at wider social and cultural issues. (2004, p. 83-4)

Constructing the Perpetrator and Victim of Domestic Violence

In a study on *Women viewing violence* (Schlesinger, Dobash, Dobash, & Weaver, 1992), women said that popular representations of social problems like domestic violence can provide a lifeline to victims/survivors of domestic violence, letting them know that they are not alone and the public is more likely to recognise and acknowledge what is a hidden abuse. Whilst such stories may seem empowering in celebrating an individual woman for escaping and surviving domestic violence, they conceal an underlying contradiction. In fact, these stories also imply that any woman who is still in a violent relationship is to blame for staying on, as the focus is clearly on what the victim should do to prevent or end the violence. The "public service notices" which often follow such reports encourage victims who have "experienced anything similar to get in touch with appropriate support agencies", but here again the burden is placed on the victim to do something about her situation, rather than focusing on the perpetrator. Domestic violence victims/survivors who read these stories when still in a violent relationship may well receive the message that they are weak for staying and that it is their *duty* to leave the relationship, thus reinforcing strong cultural messages. It is quite common to hear people saying, "Why on earth do they stay, I would walk out at the first sign of violence!"

A further, important issue in terms of domestic violence "survival" stories is whose victim/survivor stories are chosen. As victims must appeal to readers, be victims who could get out and be responsible, journalists rarely write about the elderly or children as victims as they cannot be held responsible for ending their abuse (Berns, 2001). "In order for their victim empowerment formula to work, the audience needs to believe that the victim can indeed be held responsible for ending her abusive situation" (Berns, 2004, p. 92). Berns cites the editor of *McCall's Magazine* (admittedly a traditional publication) as saying:

> I would say other criteria we take into consideration in selecting people to be covered in the magazine is [*sic*] probably not the poor, not with awful backgrounds, and this is my own personal opinion, but not those who are too fat or ugly ... readers find it very easy to distance themselves from someone who has had a less than utopian life. So we're doing a story about a woman who was abused, I can't imagine us doing a story about a woman who was a drug user and abused, because we know from letters that readers would say, "What did she expect?" (cited in Berns, 2004, p. 92)

As with the reporting of other crime stories, victims/survivors must be "appropriate victims", fitting into traditional norms of femininity to appeal to readers. "The meaning systems that we apply to the category 'crime' are metaphoric systems; the coherence and consistency of their application operates to sustain certain relations: relationships of similarity/otherness and inclusion/exclusion most commonly" (Brown, 2003, p. 45). When we look at gender and public discourse, it is not just "Benchmark Man" (Thornton, 1995) we need to be aware of. We need to be aware too of the invisible "Benchmark Woman", the white, heterosexual, able-bodied, irrational, middle class, sexed-female body, whose image and character "other" women are judged against. "Benchmark Woman" and the metaphors of respectable femininity are incredibly powerful in dividing the social world into the acceptable and non-acceptable behaviours for women.

Constructing the Perpetrator and Victim of Domestic Violence

Reactions to domestic violence victims often flow from myths attributed to those who suffer it, a separation of "them" from "us". As a result, female victims are often viewed by the public as somehow to blame, in some way unable to treat men properly or to deal with them assertively. However, this was not the finding of the research on domestic violence that I carried out, as the women participants took many actions and overcame multiple obstacles in moving through and away from abusive and violent relationships (Wilcox, 2006). Overall, the characterisation of the victim in print media sources is narrow and restrictive, one which is partially responsible for shaping a broad public acceptance that domestic violence against some victims might be deserved.

To date, there has been relatively little academic investigation into the topic of male perpetrators of domestic violence (e.g. Hester & Westmarland, 2006). The social problem of domestic violence has been largely studied and acted upon by feminist researchers and activists and traditionally the focus has been on female victims. When we turn to look at media reporting of domestic violence, it is then not surprising that media discourse rarely if ever focuses on the perpetrators. Where perpetrators are covered, it is often in the context of celebrity stories in which, as Boyle (2005, p. 87) points out, the discourses tend to follow the pattern of "sin and redemption/confession and counselling" narratives or the perpetrators tend to be constructed as sick and maladjusted individuals (McDonald, 1999).

Especially, it is interesting to contrast Bern's work on women's magazines with the utter lack of work on men's magazines. As Berns (2001) has argued, women's magazines have focused considerably on "domestic violence survival stories" over the last twenty years. In contrast, men's magazines appear not to address the issue of domestic violence at all. Is it the case that those in the media believe their readers do not want to read about male abusers? Is it not upbeat and empowering enough or is it considered too depressing for readers to tackle (Berns, 2001)? Are journalists concerned about legal issues with respect to domestic violence perpetrators? Or is it because, if the media were to focus on male perpetrators of domestic violence, they would be forced to address issues of male power and sexism that permeate our society (Berns, 2001)? This area is one that is even more under-researched than coverage of domestic violence in women's magazines and one that urgently needs further research.

The Sun newspaper, it could be argued, has provided some exceptions to the points raised above. *The Sun* has run campaigns against domestic violence since 2000 and most recently ran a series of articles by Sandra Horley, the Chief Executive of the anti-domestic violence charity Refuge. Since Rebekah Wade took over as editor of *The Sun* in January, 2003, the paper has run several high profile "name and shame" campaigns, including campaigns against paedophiles and yobs. As editor of *The Sun*, Wade was responsible for the "Shop a Yob" campaign, designed to name and shame young people who are subject to anti-social behaviour orders. *The Sun* also ran a "name and shame" campaign against domestic violence, with photographs of male perpetrators on its front page. The headline read: *Domestic Violence. Shock Issue. Once these men had enough charm to win a woman's heart. But they grew into brutes capable of a sickening crime. They're all … wife beaters and we're exposing them today* (*The Sun*, 2003, September 22).

However, this kind of coverage may not be the most helpful in addressing the issue of perpetration of domestic violence. This is in all ways a punitive campaign that individualises this social problem once again by labelling

particular men. The purpose of "naming and shaming" is
hardly about finding ways to address domestic violence in
a productive way. There are many other ways in which
newspapers and magazines could address the issue of
domestic violence perpetrators without taking a "naming
and shaming" approach. It is a serious criticism of men's
magazines that they are clearly failing to address the issue
of domestic violence and thus failing to tackle the gender-
based violence that it represents.

Public opinion on domestic violence

As stated in the introduction to this paper, public policy,
and to some extent attitudes, on domestic violence have
been shifting in the UK over the last ten years. What was
once largely accepted behaviour is less tolerated now and
some aspects of domestic violence are recognised in law as
a crime. However, despite such progress, most people
continue to tolerate abusive behaviours by men against
their female partners, because they continue to see
domestic violence as a private matter; and some consider
that, unless there are visible physical injuries, intervention
is unjustified (Berns, 2004). Also, some people actually
condone the use of domestic violence in specific contexts,
as "one in five young men and one in ten young women
think violence towards a partner is acceptable in certain
circumstances" (Burton, Kitzinger, Kelly, & Regan, 1998).

Sexual Assault Research, a survey of UK citizens run
by Amnesty International (2005) on sexual abuse (which is
often part of domestic violence) found that:

- "Blame culture" attitudes exist about women and rape;

- More than a quarter (26%) thought that a woman was partially or totally responsible for being raped if wearing sexy or revealing clothing;

- More than 1 in 5 (22%) held the same view if a woman had had many sexual partners;

- Around 1 in 12 people (8%) believed a woman was totally responsible for being raped if she had had many sexual partners;

- More than a quarter of people (30%) said a woman was partially or totally responsible for being raped if she was drunk, and more than a third (37%) held the same view if the woman had failed to say "no" clearly to the man.

More research is needed into public attitudes towards domestic violence in order to evaluate to what extent the general public retains negative and/or blaming attitudes towards some groups of female victims of domestic violence. At the same time, there is very little data on attitudes towards perpetrators of domestic violence.

Lack of gendered analyses

Conceptualising domestic violence as gendered, as primarily male violence against women in the home and a different experience from domestic violence experienced by men, clearly brings into question existing ahistorical gender-neutral stances. As domestic violence is increasingly being mainstreamed, feminist understandings based on a history of gender relations may be distorted through gender-neutral definitions and discourses. I would agree with Radford (2003, p. 33), who argues that there is a "contemporary and worrying trend of representing domestic violence as a gender-neutral, equal opportunities issue through attempts to signify 'male victimhood' and construct the female perpetrator". Certainly, there has

always been a problem in the way in which print media
cover domestic violence; that is, taking a non-gendered or
gender-neutral approach in almost all cases when covering
stories on domestic violence. Berns's qualitative analysis of
men's and political publications identified two main
discursive strategies in media resistance to feminist
constructions of the social problem of domestic violence:
"degendering the problem and gendering the blame". The
media is clearly productive in the ways in which it
constructs gender in relation to violence (Berns, 2001,
2004).

Concluding remarks

> Interrogating and challenging the nature of these representations is
> therefore one way in which critics can question – and ultimately
> change – the meanings and rewards attached to violence in our
> society. (Boyle, 2005, p. 49)

Feminists have challenged the dominant construction
of male violence in the home as private and personal. In
the 1970s and 1980s, feminists researched into, and
campaigned against, all forms of violence against women,
at the same time developing networks of refuges/shelters
and other support services. This work brought a new
discourse on male violence against women into the public
arena, providing "a vehicle for change" (Dobash &
Dobash, 1992). However, whilst feminist discourse has
emerged into the public sphere, such discourse is open to
being reshaped and sometimes distorted by the media.
Whilst the media may be useful in championing
appropriate cases of individual victims, there is a decided

reluctance to enter into more complex debates about domestic violence (Bindel, Cook & Kelly, 1995, pp. 74-75).

I argued here that the focus on the most severe and exceptional violence, with graphic imagery, hides the everyday abuse and violence suffered, which is the majority case – this makes it very difficult for many female victims to see themselves as suffering domestic violence; only some women are seen as appropriate victims. It also characterises perpetrators of domestic violence as monsters, rather than seeing them as men who draw on a cultural resource of violence against women. Demonising those men who are domestically violent allows many more men to perpetuate their abusive and controlling behaviours.

Meyers (1997, p. 19) proposes that news reporting "supports the dominant power structure by creating a consensus that appears grounded in everyday reality". Rather than challenging mainstream views, crime news reinforces certain forms of social control, with the depiction of "crime, criminals, and victims changing over time to correspond with social, political, and economic changes in society" (Meyers, p. 21). In Meyers's view, news reporting thus operates hegemonically, to privilege certain discourses about violence against women over others. Unhelpful media responses deny or minimise domestic violence and blame women directly or indirectly; helpful support responses attempt to shift the discourse of blame away from victims.

To a great extent, the press sets the frame for both the quantity and the quality of public discourse on specific issues in public life, including crime and social welfare. In this case, the quantity of reporting on domestic violence is minimal and the quality is distorted in the way it covers victims only and for the most part fails to address perpetrators. However, media participation does not go in

one direction only; readers often engage actively and
intelligently with print media reports, bringing their own
experiences, values and attitudes formed over their lifetime
in relation to other institutions and people. Press
representations of the issues surrounding domestic
violence must hence be acknowledged as an influential
part of an ongoing cycle, and individual journalists and
editors be seen as both products of, and participants in, the
very society they seek to inform (Evans, 2001). Ultimately,
"If we want to see a change in the way that our media
reports crime, we need to lobby for a change in the way
our politicians talk about crime" (Garside, 2003).

References

Amnesty International (2005). *UK: New poll finds a third of
people believe women who flirt partially responsible for being
raped.* Retrieved July 10, 2007, from:
http://www.amnesty.org.uk/news_details.asp?NewsI
D=16618.

Berns, N. (1999). "My problem and how I solved it":
Domestic violence in women's magazines. *The
Sociological Quarterly, 40* (1), 85-108.

Berns, N. (2001). Degendering the problem and gendering
the blame: Political discourse on women and violence.
Gender & Society, 15 (2), 262-281.

Berns, N. (2004). *Framing the victim: Domestic violence, media,
and social problems.* Hawthorne, NY: Aldine de Gruyter.

Bindel, J., Cook, K., & Kelly, L. (1995). Trials and tribulations – *Justice for Women*: A campaign for the 90s. In G. Griffin (Ed.), *Feminist activism in the 1990s* (pp. 65-76). London: Taylor & Francis.

Boyle, K. (2005). *Media and violence: Gendering the debates*. London: Sage.

Brown, S. (2003). *Crime and law in media culture*. Buckingham: Open University Press.

Burman, M., Brown, J., & Batchelor, S. (2003). "Taking it to heart": Girls and the meanings of violence. In E. Stanko (Ed.), *The meanings of violence* (pp. 71-89). London: Routledge.

Burton, S., Kitzinger, J., Kelly, L., & Regan, L. (1998). *Young people's attitudes to violence, sex and relationships: A survey and focus group study*. Edinburgh: Zero Tolerance Charitable Trust.

Dobash, R. E., & Dobash, R. P. (1992). *Women, violence, and social change*. London: Routledge.

Evans, L. (2001). Desperate lovers and wanton women: Press representations of domestic violence. *Hecate, 27* (2), 147-174.

Flood-Page, C., & Taylor, J. (Eds.). (2003). *Crime in England and Wales, 2001/2002: Supplementary volume*. London:

Constructing the Perpetrator and Victim of Domestic Violence

Home Office Research, Development and Statistics Directorate.

Gallagher, M. (2004). The impact of monitoring media images of women. In C. Carter & L. Steiner (Eds.), *Critical readings: Media and gender* (pp. 148-161). Maidenhead: Open University Press.

Garside, R. (2003, November 19). *Media and crime: Speech to Nacro Conference.* Retrieved May 30, 2008, from: http://www.crimeandjustice.org.uk/opus340.html?search_string=sex%20crime%20and%20the%20media.

Greer, C. (2003). *Sex crime and the media: Sex offending and the press in a divided society.* Cullompton: Willan.

Hester, M., & Westmarland, N. (2006). *Service provision for perpetrators of domestic violence.* Retrieved May 30, 2008, from: http://www.bristol.ac.uk/sps/downloads/FPCW/serviceprovisionreport.pdf

Home Office. (2005). *Domestic violence: A national report.* Retrieved May 30, 2008, from: http://www.crimereduction.homeoffice.gov.uk/domesticviolence/domesticviolence51.pdf

Jewkes, Y. (2004). Media representations of criminal justice. In J. Muncie & D. Wilson (Eds.), *Student handbook of criminal justice and criminology* (pp. 67-79). London: Cavendish Publishing.

Kirkwood, C. (1993). *Leaving abusive partners: From the scars of survival to the wisdom for change.* London: Sage.

McDonald, M. G. (1999). Unnecessary roughness: Gender and racial politics in domestic violence media events. *Sociology of Sport Journal, 16,* 111-133.

Meyers, M. (1994). News of battering. *Journal of Communication, 44* (2), 47-63.

Meyers, M. (1997). *News coverage of violence against women: Engendering blame.* Thousand Oaks, CA: Sage.

Naffine, N. (1996). *Feminism and criminology.* Philadelphia: Temple University Press.

Naylor, B. (2001). Reporting violence in the British print media: Gendered stories. *Howard Journal of Criminal Justice, 40* (2), 180-194.

Pain, R. (1999). Women's experiences of violence over the life-course. In E. K. Teather (Ed.), *Embodied geographies: Spaces, bodies and rites of passage* (pp. 126-141). London: Routledge.

Radford, J. (2003). Professionalising responses to domestic violence in the UK: Definitional debates. *Community Safety Journal, 2* (1), 32-39.

Schlesinger, P., Dobash, R. E., Dobash, R. P., & Weaver, K.
(1992). *Women viewing violence.* London: British Film
Institute.

Spector, M., & Kitsuse, J. I. (1987). *Constructing social
problems.* (New ed.). Menlo Park, CA: Cummings;
Hawthorne, NY: Aldine de Gruyter. (Originally
published 1977).

Stanko, E. A. (2001). The day to count: Reflections on a
methodology to raise awareness about the impact of
domestic violence in the UK. *Criminology and Criminal
Justice, 1* (2), 215-226.

The Sun. (2003, September 22). The brutes are exposed.

Surette, R. (1998). *Media, crime, and criminal justice: Images
and realities.* (2nd ed.). Belmont, CA: Wadsworth.
(Originally published 1992).

Thornton, M. (Ed.). (1995). *Public and private: Feminist legal
debates.* Melbourne: Oxford University Press.

United Nations (1995). *Fourth World Conference on Women:
Beijing Declaration.* Retrieved August 28, 2005, from:
http://www.un.org/womenwatch/daw/beijing/platf
orm/declar.htm.

Walby, S., & Allen, J. (2004). *Domestic violence, sexual assault
and stalking: Findings from the British Crime Survey.*

London: Home Office.

Wilcox, P. (2006). *Surviving domestic violence: Gender, poverty and agency.* Basingstoke: Palgrave Macmillan.

Wilcox, P. (2007). Survivors of domestic violence, community and care. In S. Balloch & M. Hill (Eds.), *Care, community and citizenship: Research and practice in a changing policy context* (pp. 121-140). Bristol: Policy Press.

World Health Organization. (2000). *Violence against women.* Retrieved June 21, 2007, from: http://www.who.int/mediacentre/factsheets/fs239/en/.

World Health Organization. (2002). *World report on violence and health.* Retrieved November 9, 2006, from: http://www.who.int/violence_injury_prevention/violence/world_report/en/.

Wykes, M. (2001). *News, crime, and culture.* London: Pluto Press.

MENTAL HEALTH AND THE MEDIA: CON(TEXTS) OF PUBLIC FEAR AND PREJUDICE

Lisa Blackman

Introduction

The experience of stigma, discrimination and prejudice for people living with mental health problems is still a pressing concern. The intractability of such problems and the secondary issues that this creates has been the focus of a range of attempts to combat public fear and prejudice. These range from calls from mental health charities, such as Mind and Mental Health Media, to challenge what tends to pass in the media as representations of mental ill health, through to concerns of government agencies to coordinate anti-stigma campaigns to normalise experiences of depression and psychosis. Strategies have included equating mental ill health to experiences of health and illness commonly understood as physical or biological in origin, and arguing that people living with mental health problems are often treated with derision and fear, rather than with compassion and sympathy. The mobilisation of the so-called "biogenetic paradigm" in such strategies has often resulted in catastrophic failure. The repositioning of mental ill health as a treatable biological or physical illness, rather than removing the moral and ethical culpability of the service user, has generated increased fears and prejudices aligned to the issue of *choice* and *responsibility*. Put simply, if a person is not responsible for their mental ill health (where responsibility is displaced to the gene or biochemical pathway overseen by the appropriate expert – usually a psychiatrist), then mental ill health is potentially more alarming, because it could erupt as a random occurrence over which the person has little or no control.

The chapter interrogates this paradoxical context in light of the increasingly sympathetic portrayal of mental ill health in Hollywood films. The chapter will consider why, despite concerted and consistent campaigns by mental health charities and government agencies to reduce public fear and prejudice, it is so difficult to change people's minds.

Violence and mental health

An established literature within media studies has begun to explore the predominant ways in which mental ill health has repeatedly been signified across different media forms and practices. One important media study, published in a British psychiatric journal, *Psychiatric Bulletin,* concerned the continual and repeated aligning of the person with mental health difficulties with violence, both towards themselves and usually towards others. Philo (1994) concluded that, across the broadcast and factual media (such as television news and print journalism), the person with mental health difficulties often becomes known to us as an object of danger, threat, fear and loathing. The mad, we are told, are disturbing, threatening, a risk, a time bomb waiting to go off. Tabloid headlines represent the mentally distressed as "Patients Who Kill" or "Insane Killers". They are evil, dangerous, sick and immoral. Mental ill health is usually linked to criminality in the context of homicide or rare incidents of violence, where there is always concern for the safety of the public rather than care for the individual involved. The mad are constructed as "other" to rationality, to be feared, avoided or shut away (either in prison or psychiatric institutions). These fears are increasingly set within damning indictments of the failure of psychiatric professionals and institutions to protect the safety of the public, owing to blunders and systemic errors in diagnosis, care and treatment.

The potential for systemic error and its adjudication is shared by the judiciary who, in cases of criminal actions, are required to decide whether a person should be held responsible for their actions (and are therefore bad) or whether they should not be held responsible, because of mental ill health. The legal system relies upon psychological and psychiatric expertise to make this distinction, by assuming that certain forms of experience are biological in nature and therefore beyond a person's control. If a person is found to be mad rather than bad, they are absolved of legal responsibility for the crime they committed. They are "other" to rationality and cannot be held responsible for their actions. This will usually result in a lesser sentence, such as manslaughter rather than murder, or it may be decided that they are not mentally fit enough to stand trial and will reside indefinitely within maximum security hospitals, such as Broadmoor.

Anti-stigma campaigns

An anti-stigma campaign run by the Royal College of Psychiatry in 2004 was screened across cinemas throughout the country, sandwiched between advertisements for consumer products and services and trailers for forthcoming films. The campaign, "Changing Minds: Every Family in the Land", is reminiscent of many others run by mental health charities and government and psychiatric agencies that aim to reduce public fear and prejudice towards people with mental health difficulties. The campaign aimed to persuade people that mental ill health is much like any other physical (chronic) illness, such as diabetes; therefore, people should not be treated with contempt and discrimination. This approach is known as the "Mental illness is an illness like any other approach"

(Read, Haslam, Sayce, & Davies, 2006). The campaign, titled "1 in 4", incorporated the message that one in eight people are likely to see a psychiatric professional at some point in their lives, and that one in four people will suffer from a mental health difficulty, including depression. Mental ill health is framed within this campaign through a biogenetic paradigm; that is, that mental ill health is the result of biochemical or neurological disturbance, located within the brain, which can be treated with pharmaceutical agents. This is despite the fact that the status of biologically-based discourses is far from reliable and that the claims of psychiatry are contradictory and incomplete (Boyle, 1990; Blackman, 2001; Gardner, 2003; Dumit, 2005; Thomas et al., 2005). The effects of psychotropic drugs used in the treatment of mental health difficulties are widely contested, as there is evidence of drugs' short and long term toxic effects rather than of their efficacy.

However, this does not stop the performative injunction to understand mental ill health through a biogenetic paradigm from having any less of a cultural effect. In this respect, the media is seen as an important site for both changing people's minds and promoting and creating fear and prejudice. As I have argued elsewhere, this paradigm forms the basis of the marketing practices of pharmaceutical companies. It is also creating what Dumit (2005) terms a process of de-psychiatrisation. This is where consumers no longer require a psychiatric diagnosis to understand their suffering as a biological disorder. He argues that the internet and television are providing sites for self-diagnosis that promote the view that mental ill health is biological in origin, leading to a form of "dependent normality". This is echoed in the promotion of such a paradigm by celebrities in Britain, including Stephen Fry, Alastair Campbell, Frank Bruno and Stuart Goddard (Adam Ant) (Blackman, 2007). Dumit (1997) has argued that the understanding that schizophrenia, for example, is biological in origin offers comfort to service users and their families and provides some protection against the stigma and shame afforded by a psychiatric diagnosis. However, it would seem that any fears and anxieties generated by such a diagnosis are difficult to assuage and that, rather than improving public fear and stigma, the reverse seems to have happened.

A recent report into the effects of anti-stigma campaigns has argued that they have actually failed, worsening rather than improving public fear and prejudice. The main reason for the failure was precisely the promotion of the biogenetic paradigm and its framing of mental ill health as a brain disease. Ironically, the person with mental health difficulties is reconfirmed, within this paradigm, as a danger. They are viewed as unable to control their behaviour and at the mercy of a biochemical disturbance. The report suggests that the biogenetic paradigm is based upon an essentialist view of human subjectivity. That is, that mental ill health is "discrete, immutable and invariably rooted in a biological abnormality" (Read et al., 2006, p. 312). This reduces the complexity of human subjectivity to what Rose (2007) terms a "molar" view of the body. This is one in which the body is defined by or composed of particular parts or preformed entities. These might include tissues, bones, limbs, blood, hormones, biochemicals, and so on.

Historical production of psychopathology as "otherness"

It seems, however, that many people do not subscribe to the view that psychopathology is "simply biological". It is more common within media and cultural studies to "think" of bodies as *processes* rather than as substances or entities that are defined through their connections with others, human and non-human (cf. Blackman, 2008). This *relational* approach to subjectivity is one that raises some rather different questions about the production of psychopathology. It particularly directs our attention to the historical conditions and discourses which have led psychopathology to be located within the singular, isolated, individualised, molar body, understood primarily through a biogenetic paradigm. This may well be because of the scientific roots of the biogenetic approach.

Michel Foucault suggested that the human sciences emerged in a historical context which led to the development of knowledge and practices that organised and became central to broader strategies of governing and managing populations (Foucault, 1971). Rose (1985) developed these ideas in relation to the psychological sciences, repositioning them through the concept of the "psy complex". The psy complex incorporates both psychology and psychiatry, which are key knowledge practices that have historically played a central role in targeting, mapping and classifying "otherness". The term otherness refers to all those differences to the fiction of autonomous selfhood which came to signify deviance, deficiency, abnormality and pathology. Thus, certain groups in the 19th century became defined by their bodies, rather than by the rationality of their minds, for example, and were viewed as "other" to civilisation and rationality (see Blackman & Walkerdine, 2001).

This "othering" process clearly applies to the "problem of psychopathology" (or madness, as it was known within the 19th century), as mental health difficulties were then viewed primarily as degenerative diseases that affected human *will*. The will was seen as a form of psychological control that allowed people to dominate their bodily instincts and desires. Diseases of degeneracy, understood as the reversion of the body to more primitive and animal forms of behaviour and experience, were viewed as *simple* forms of madness that were linked to an inferior biological constitution. This was seen to result primarily in a disease of the will, which would allow base bodily instincts to dominate the mind, resulting in mental and physical pathology. This view is illustrated in the following quotation from a famous British psychiatrist:

> The formation of a character, in which the thoughts, feelings and actions are under the habitual guidance of a well-fashioned will, is perhaps the highest effort of self-development. It represents the attainment, by conscious method, of a harmony between man and nature; a condition in which the individual has succeeded in making the best of himself, of the human nature with which he has to do, and of the world in which he moves and has his being. (Maudsley, 1874, p. 300)

Within this paradigm, simple forms of madness were also associated with the bodies of women, with colonial subjects, with the working classes and with people with different sexualities. Within psychopathology as a disease of degeneracy, certain groups of people were viewed as closer to the animal and the primitive. Women were viewed as having an inherently weak constitution (as were the working classes, people with different sexualities and colonial subjects) that predisposed them to disorders of will. Thus, the emerging biogenetic paradigm was itself always cross-cut by classed, gendered, racialised and sexualised forms of thinking. Psychopathology was linked to the inability to exercise the will, aligned with a disease process within the brain of certain categories of people. For Maudsley, as for many other psychiatrists of the time, the ability to develop the will was limited by inherited constitution. This discourse portrayed certain bodies as abject and "other" to a specified norm. Let us examine the following arguments made by the British psychiatrist Henry Maudsley:

> The common system of female education, which is now falling fast to pieces, was ill-adapted to store the mind with useful knowledge, and to train up a strong character; had it been designed specifically to heighten emotional sensibility and to weaken reason, it could hardly have been more fitted to produce that effect. Its whole tendency has been to increase that predominance of the affective life in woman, which she owes mainly to her sexual constitution.
>
> (Maudsley, 1879, p. 166)

In his argument against the provision of female education, women are seen to be more prone to "simple" forms of psychopathology, owing to what was taken to be their inferior biological constitution. This is not to say that white, middle-class men were not seen to suffer from psychopathology, but that the forms this would take were seen to be more *complex* and linked to their *intellectual* rather than their *affective* life. *Complex* forms of psychopathology were aligned to the overstretched mind and were usually seen to be the province of the white middle-class man. These were viewed as forms of *moral* rather than *biological* insanity and were linked to reasoning that had gone awry in some way. They were constituted as conditions of poetic fire (Porter, 1987) that linked psychopathology to creative genius. Complex forms of psychopathology were equated to dream processes that allowed the person to make new and novel connections. This could produce the potential for both the absurdity of delusional thought and occasionally the creative genius of the innovative association.

The debate about the links between psychopathology and creativity continues to this day. Raj Persaud, the celebrity psychiatrist, gave a public lecture on this topic in 2006, and the theme formed the backdrop to a recent exhibition at the Whitechapel Gallery in London on "Outsider Art", or what used to be known as "Art of the Insane" (Thompson, 2006). One of the discussions in relation to the artworks exhibited at the gallery was whether the works should be accorded some kind of diagnostic significance (for example, exhibiting signs and symptoms of the person's mental pathology), or whether they were expressions of creative genius. This Romantic view of psychopathology saw madness as a state that would allow access to hidden realms that were not usually accessible. This equated the psychiatric patient to a voyager going on a journey into landscapes that were denied to those who were seen to be governed by social rules and convention or, in the psychiatric terms we have been discussing, the action of the will. The mad were to become exalted and celebrated as those who were able to live beyond or outside the norms of bourgeois culture, unfettered by social constraint. Rather than being considered degenerate, the "mad" were to become the object of a set of desires, fetishes and fascinations that produced them as heroes inhabiting the borderlands of creative genius.

Film and psychopathology

What I now consider is how this classed, sexed, gendered and raced distinction between *simple* and *complex* psychopathology is reactivated in the contemporary media. It would seem that these understandings, which derive from a differentiation between forms of psychopathology considered moral and aligned to the mind and those that were considered biological and located within the body, have not been left behind. In Hollywood's apparently sympathetic portrayal of people with mental health difficulties, psychopathology is not simply reproduced as an object of fear, derision and loathing. However, distinctions between simple and complex and masculine and feminine are still very much a central motif in the gendered differentiations which underpin rather different genres of film. Let us start this comparison by focusing upon a genre of Hollywood films which have aligned psychopathology to creative genius. These films include *As Good As It Gets* (Brooks, 1997), *Shine* (Hicks, 1996), and *A Beautiful Mind* (Howard, 2001). These representations of the "psychopathological other" as a hero refer to men who experience mental distress owing to their creative genius. In *As Good As It Gets,* the central character, played by Jack Nicholson, is a novelist who is plagued by obsessional forms of behaviour akin to the psychiatric category known as Obsessive Compulsive Disorder. In *Shine,* the life of the concert pianist David Helfgott is portrayed through aligning his creative genius to autism. In *A Beautiful Mind,* the life of the Nobel Prize winner, John Nash, played by Russell Crowe, is also plagued by psychosis and obsessional delusions, which link his creative mathematic genius to psychopathology. The narrative structure of these Hollywood scripts follows a similar path. The heroes experience mental distress and, usually through the love of a good woman, they are eventually able to accept their experiences as signs of illness. Through this support, they embark on a journey of recovery, usually aided by psychotropic drugs. They eventually receive public recognition for their genius through a series of accolades. The men become heroes through their struggles, which end in public recognition of their talents.

In these Hollywood representations, there is a certain romanticisation of psychopathology, in which it is linked to creativity, to transgressiveness and to eccentricity. The sufferers are constructed as heroes rather than as victims. Their psychopathology is aligned to their capacity for rational thought located within the mind, which has gone awry, allowing creative novel connections as well as delusional obsessions. Let us compare these with representations of female psychopathology, which take a rather different form and expression. In films such as *Serial Mom* (Waters, 1994), *The Hand that Rocks the Cradle* (Hanson, 1992), *Basic Instinct* (Verhoeven, 1992), and *Single White Female* (Schroeder, 1992), female psychopathology is expressed through violence, usually towards others, and is seen to be located and expressed through the body rather than the mind. This is often also a body that is primarily sexualised and seen to be driven by irrational and often unsated desire. The narrative structure of these films also differs from those we have already compared. The women are constructed as objects of danger, threat and fear and the ending is one in which the women, who are constituted as psychopathic killers, are killed off, imprisoned or punished.

The women's actions are all linked to irrationality, desire or passion, which is aligned to their unstable female biological and sexed constitution. The central characters of the films – Peyton, the nanny in *The Hand that Rocks the Cradle* and Annie, the surrogate mother in *Misery* (Reiner, 1990), for example – express a psychopathology which is constituted as irrationality through violence. The narrative resolution in both films is the killing off of these female characters so that calm can be restored. These representations of the female *psychopathological other* are radically different from those portraying masculinity and male psychopathology. The women do not become heroes. Rather, they become victims of their own biological constitution, as they are unable to recognise their experiences as signs of illness. They are seen to lack any insight, which adds to their dangerousness. They are constituted as objects of fear and loathing, rather than objects of envy, desire and fascination.

John Waters, the American film director of *Serial Mom*, has provided a camp, ironic comedy of such a trope, in which the central character, played by Kathleen Turner, embodies all of the motifs which are endlessly circulated in media representations of female psychopathology. The camera continually uses body shots and minute shots of facial expressions to signify her psychopathology, which is expressed through brutal and senseless acts of violence towards others. Her psychopathology is literally seen to be written on the body, with her affective and emotional instability and fragility particularly expressed through her eyes. The link of the eyes to female psychopathology is one that has also endured within more factual media representations. One only has to think of the iconic images of Myra Hindley or Rosemary West and the way in which their psychopathology and evilness were seen to be given away by their cold, staring eyes (see Blackman & Walkerdine, 2001). Of course, there are exceptions to both of these genres; one can perhaps think of films such as *Sylvia* (Jeffs, 2003) and *The Hours* (Daldry, 2002), which portray the lives of the female writers Sylvia Plath and Virginia Woolf and provide more complicated versions of their psychopathology and its links to creative genius. These films certainly deserve more attention for the ways in which they both confirm and reject such dominant motifs at different points in the narratives (see Blackman, 2004, for a discussion of *The Hours*).

"Rehearsal of Memory"

The artist Graham Harwood produced an interactive digital art piece (a CD-ROM) which explores what stories get told about such individuals and what is silenced, suppressed and allowed to fall into oblivion. The artwork, titled *Rehearsal of Memory*, is based upon the lives of six maximum security prisoners at Ashworth Maximum Security Psychiatric Hospital. Many of those who took part in this artwork have killed or maimed; the horror or atrocity of their crimes silence their own stories of private suffering and humiliation. The aim of the artwork is to allow the user to engage with the stories of these individuals that are usually repressed, as they are known to the public only through their outward displays of hostility and violence. The artwork is made up of a composite image of a masculine body created from digital scans of the bodies of the men taking part in the piece. What results is an anonymous, disquieting image, which retains the anonymity of the men involved (a requirement of the institution), but contains traces of the individual men's lives and the traces that remain as ghostly hauntings of stories never told. The user is confronted with a body covered with scars and tattoos. Users can navigate around the body and click on any of the markings to be confronted with a hidden story relating to one of the inmates' lives. These are stories of sexual abuse, emotional abuse, torture, humiliation and accompanying feelings of hate, anger, frustration, guilt and depression. If you linger too long on the stories, a tabloid headline flashes up showing how such individuals would tend to be represented in the media as "Psychiatric Killers" or "Insane Killers". The following are examples of such stories, which reveal the men's retreat into their own bodies in order to express something of their lives and the humiliation and inadequacy they have been made to feel:

> This was the worst I'd ever cut up before. I cut open my old appendix wound, stuck pins on the inside of the wound and swallowed a broken light bulb.

> When I was younger I didn't like myself and I still don't. The reasons for this were because in some way I blamed myself for what had happened to me and my sister. My Father was, and is, a monster.

In previous writing, I discussed the significance of this artwork and suggested how we might rethink psychopathology in the light of the complex stories disclosed by this work (Blackman, 1998). One suggestion was to focus on the difficulties the men have in living masculine images of control and autonomy when their lives have produced an economy of affect and emotion, which creates feelings of fragility and persecution rather than a sense of control and worth. This is not to condone their actions, but rather to expose a normative image that we are all continually invited to judge, inspect and, in relation to which, act upon ourselves. Rose (1996) has termed this regulative image or ideal the "fiction of autonomous selfhood", a norm or regime of personhood in which we are required to experience ourselves as whole, unified, coherent, clearly bounded and separate from others. We are invited to experience success and failure as being down to our own choices and the decisions we have made across almost all aspects of our lives. There are costs and benefits attached to this fiction; potentially, it can create its own psychopathology for those who, for a myriad of reasons, find this ideal difficult to inhabit and embody. The complexities of this approach for dealing with psychopathology and its media representation are somewhat at odds with the biogenetic paradigm.

Conclusion

The contemporary media's focus both on portrayals of psychopathology deemed to be more sympathetic and on an invitation by mental health charities and governmental agencies to try and lessen public fear and prejudice, rather than promote and produce it, appears to be at a crossroads. The (con)texts of the media's production of psychopathology tell us something about why certain motifs and discourses recur, and also perhaps why it is so difficult to change people's minds. Foucault (1971) suggested that any history of the present needs to engage with the discourses that have combined and recombined to produce what passes as norms and common sense and with which some ways of life have become naturalised and normalised. We can clearly see that the fiction of autonomous selfhood emerged as a norm through the way in which certain people were made "other" to this desired ideal and became excluded from rationality and civilisation. The framing of psychopathology through a biogenetic paradigm retains and reactivates the singular molar body, primarily understood through the brain, as a central discourse which confirms this fiction as natural and normal. It also positions people differentially in relation to this regulatory ideal, with gender, class, race and sexuality still significant ways in which what are now understood as neurotic and psychotic distinctions in psychopathology are made salient. What links Hollywood representations and campaigns to reduce stigma in relation to mental health problems is the reliance on a biogenetic paradigm. This is significant even if the distinction between more simple and complex forms of psychopathology is given a gendered twist. Perhaps the work of digital artists such as Graham Harwood gives us some clues as to what stories must and need to be told if we are to expose these contexts for what they are: historically contingent and therefore mutable ways of specifying, understanding and even producing psychopathology in all its modern forms.

References

Blackman, L. (1998). Culture, technology and subjectivity: An 'ethical' analysis. In J. Wood (Ed.), *The virtual embodied: Presence/practice/technology* (pp. 132-146). London: Routledge.

Blackman, L. (2001). *Hearing voices: Embodiment and experience.* London: Free Association Books.

Blackman, L. (2004). Self-help, media cultures and the production of female psychopathology. *European Journal of Cultural Studies, 7* (2), 219-236.

Blackman, L. (2007). Psychiatric culture and bodies of resistance. *Body & Society, 13* (2), 1-23.

Blackman, L. (2008). *The body: The key concepts.* Oxford: Berg.

Blackman, L., & Walkerdine, V. (2001). *Mass hysteria: Critical psychology and media studies.* Basingstoke: Palgrave.

Mental Health and the Media

Boyle, M. (1990). *Schizophrenia: A scientific delusion?* London: Routledge.

Brooks, J. L. (Director/Producer). (1997). *As good as it gets* [Motion picture]. United States: TriStar Pictures/Gracie Films.

Daldry, S. (Director). (2002). *The hours* [Motion picture]. United States: Paramount Pictures/Miramax Films/Scott Rudin Productions.

Dumit, J. (1997). A digital image of the category of the person: PET scanning and objective self-fashioning. In G. L. Downey & J. Dumit (Eds.), *Cyborgs and citadels: Anthropological interventions in emerging sciences and technologies* (pp. 83-102). Santa Fe, NM: School of American Research Press.

Dumit, J. (2005). The de-psychiatrisation of mental illness. *Journal of Public Mental Health, 4* (3), 8-13.

Foucault, M. (1971) *Madness and civilization: A history of insanity in the age of reason* (R. Howard, Trans.). London: Tavistock. (Original work published 1961).

Gardner, P. (2003). Distorted packaging: Marketing depression as illness, drugs as cure. *Journal of Medical Humanities, 24* (1-2), 105-130.

Hanson, C. (Director). (1992). *The hand that rocks the cradle* [Motion picture]. United States: Hollywood Pictures/ Interscope Communications/Nomura Babcock & Brown.

Harwood, G. (1995). *Rehearsal of memory* [CD-ROM]. London: Book Works; London: Artec.

Hicks, S. (Director). (1996). *Shine* [Motion picture]. Australia: Australian Film Finance Corporation/Film Victoria; United States: Momentum Films.

Howard, R. (Director/Producer). (2001). *A beautiful mind* [Motion picture]. United States: Columbia Pictures/DreamWork SKG/Imagine Entertainment.

Jeffs, C. (Director). (2003). *Sylvia* [Motion picture]. United Kingdom: British Broadcasting Corporation/British Film Council/Capitol Films/Ruby Films; United States: Focus Features.

Maudsley, H. (1874). *Responsibility in mental disease.* London: Henry S. King & Co.

Maudsley, H. (1879). *The pathology of mind. London:* Macmillan.

Persaud, R. (2006). *Creativity and mental illness: Do you have to be mad to be creative?* [Gresham College public lecture, delivered November 8, 2006]. Retrieved April 1, 2008, from:

http://www.gresham.ac.uk/event.asp?PageId=45&Ev
entId=561

Philo, G. (1994). Media images and popular beliefs. *Psychiatric Bulletin, 18* (3), 173-174.

Porter, R. (1987). *Mind-forg'd manacles: A history of madness in England from the Restoration to the Regency.* London: Athlone Press.

Read, J., Haslam, N., Sayce, L., & Davies, E. (2006). Prejudice and schizophrenia: A review of the 'mental illness is an illness like any other' approach. *Acta Psychiatrica Scandinavica, 14* (5), 303-318.

Reiner, R. (Director/Producer). (1990). *Misery* [Motion picture]. United States: Castle Rock Entertainment/ Nelson Entertainment.

Rose, N. (1985). *The psychological complex: Psychology, politics and society in England, 1869-1939.* London: Routledge & Kegan Paul.

Rose, N. (1996). *Inventing our selves: Psychology, power, and personhood.* Cambridge: Cambridge University Press.

Rose, N. (2007). *The politics of life itself: Biomedicine, power, and subjectivity in the twenty-first century.* Princeton, NJ: Princeton University Press.

Schroeder, B. (Director/Producer). (1992). *Single White female* [Motion picture]. United States: Columbia Pictures Corporation.

Thomas, P., Bracken, P., Cutler, P., Hayward, R., May, R., & Yasmeen, S. (2005). Challenging the globalisation of biomedical psychiatry. *Journal of Public Mental Health, 4* (3), 23-32.

Thompson, J. (Curator). (2006). *Inner worlds outside* [Exhibition, 28 April – 25 June]. London: Whitechapel Art Gallery.

Verhoeven, P. (Director). (1992). *Basic instinct* [Motion picture]. France: Canal+; United States: Carolco Pictures/TriStar Pictures.

Waters, J. (Director). (1994). *Serial mom* [Motion picture]. United States: Polar Entertainment Corporation.

THE MEDIA AND ILLICIT DRUG USE: FAIRY TALES FOR THE EARLY 21ST CENTURY?

Adrian Barton

Introduction

The tabloid press has a fascination with all things "celebrity": we are allowed to examine the minutiae of their lives and often asked to "take sides" when this or that relationship flounders or flourishes. For example, examine the following headlines and passages from the tabloid press concerning the actions of the "celebrity couple" Kate Moss and Pete Doherty:

> Junkie rocker Pete Doherty ... notorious for his sick "blood paintings". (*Daily Star*, 2006, September 11)

> Kate Moss wrote several lines of poetry about her miserable love life with junkie Pete Doherty. In it, she says drugs ruined their relationship.... Kate – who dumped Doherty over his filthy drug habit – scrawled the passage in his shabby journal. (*The Sun*, 2006, June 30)

> Kate Moss to "rescue" Pete Doherty from Drugs Hell. (*SoFeminine.co.uk*, 2006, March 17)

Arguably, these quotes, which are representative of the 114,000 plus results which can be obtained by typing "Kate Moss and Pete Doherty" into Google, illustrate the tabloids' fascination and reportage of illicit drug use. Whilst at first glance they are clearly reporting on what appears to be a turbulent relationship between two high-profile people, closer inspection makes it is possible to see the essential nature of a fairy or morality tale in the headlines: an essentially good young man becomes

119

spellbound and subsequently enslaved, turning him into a frightful and destructive ogre. A beautiful young woman falls in love with the ogre, despite the fact that he is tarnished, and predictably that love does not run smoothly. All the advice she gets from her family and the local villagers implore her to end the relationship, because the ogre is beyond redemption. She rejects this advice because, despite despairing over their future, she knows that she can break the spell simply by offering and giving her love.

As in the fairy stories we are all so familiar with, there is a clear dichotomy in the reporting, with a distinction between "bad Pete" and "poor Kate"; this paper argues that such unrealistic divisions between ogres and innocents serve to form public opinion and ultimately set the tone for any subsequent debate concerning our approach to dealing with illicit drug use. As a consequence, despite having reached a stage in Britain when we need a major overhaul of our approach to illicit drug use, we may be unable to enter into a mature debate because the majority of the information obtained by the general public fails to rise far above the level of fairy tales (Barton, 2003). This is due to the four interrelated factors:

1. The legacy of the "British System" on illicit drug policy;

2. The fact that "There is no such thing as a neutral drug policy..." (Blackman 2004, p. 187);

3. A shift in public morality; and

4. The role which the media plays in shaping perceptions of crime and, indeed, in the case of the tabloids, the cultural discourse of the 21st century.

This paper will explore the manner in which those four factors enable the tabloids' dichotomous views to dominate representations of drug use. It begins by looking at the British System and the manner in which it has developed. Particular attention is paid to the role of morality and culture in the shaping of the British approach to illicit drug use. From there, the paper moves to explore perceptions of illicit drug use in present-day Britain. It offers a brief overview of the manner in which illicit drug use is portrayed in the media. It then moves to argue that, amongst a significant minority of the population, illicit drug taking has become a "crime of everyday life" (Felson, 2002), which makes media representations unrealistic in terms of the majority of illicit drug use in contemporary Britain. The paper will conclude by suggesting that, given the media's obsession with sensationalism and titillation, it blocks a much needed debate about the future direction of illicit drug policy.

The British System

Although the history of the British System has been covered extensively (Barton [2003]; Berridge [2005], amongst many others), it is worth a brief review of its origins in order to understand better contemporary approaches to illicit drug use. Berridge (2005, p. 7) identifies three "British Systems": the lay/commercial system which held sway until the middle part of the nineteenth century; the pharmaceutical regulation system, which dominated from the mid-nineteenth century until the onset of the First World War; and the medico-penal system, legitimated by Rolleston in 1926. Briefly, Rolleston allowed the prescription of maintenance doses by doctors, but also allowed the criminal justice system to punish drug users who were using substances illicitly. Rolleston set in train our present-day approach. The three systems have distinctive characteristics, and it is important to focus on the reasons behind the paradigm shifts and change due to shifts in morality and culture.

Before the onset of modern medicine, treatment of illnesses was dependent on lay remedies and herbal cures, passed down from generation to generation (Coleman, 1985). The lay/commercial system can be seen as a continuation of those practices. Even where doctors were available, the level of public trust in the abilities of "sawbones" was low: this, coupled with the prohibitive cost of official health care, meant that the majority of the population self-medicated. By the turn of the 1700s, opium was the drug of choice: a freely available and very effective "cure-all". Opium was imported into Britain legally from Turkey and was then distributed throughout the country, often in the form of laudanum or other opiate-based preparations, and sold in grocery stores and quite literally off the back of wagons by hawkers and peddlers (Berridge, 2005).

Thus, as Barton (2003, p. 8) notes, "opiate use was not the subject of moral opprobrium" during this period. Indeed, opium was used as iprobrufen- and paracetamol-based products are used today, with the majority of households having opium-based products in their store cupboards. It is equally important to note that the British state had no interest or indeed ability to control the use of opium, even though accidental overdosing was commonplace. Indeed, Hooker (1996) argues that control of opium would have been counterproductive and morally unacceptable, because of the economic importance of opium to Britain at this time. Hooker emphasises this by likening British opium traders to the drug cartels of the twentieth century. Clearly, even up to the middle of the 1800s, the lay/commercial system was simply continuing a social and moral tradition of self-medication that had been in place for centuries before.

However, by around the mid-1800s, moral, social and cultural shifts were beginning to take place which impacted on how opiates and other substances were both viewed and employed. There were two main reasons for this. First were scientific developments in medicine and the onset of modern treatment and drugs, which supplanted the reliance on opium as a cure-all. In turn, this led to a growth in the availability of doctors and a surge in public confidence in their ability to provide effective treatment as doctors and professionals. Technological advances, such as the hypodermic syringe, also saw the rapidly professionalising medics claim ownership of certain substances and their uses.

The second reason for the shift was a growing concern over the morality of the working class and the susceptibility of the deserving poor to corruption by all manner of evils. This is an important development, as it is at this point that morality enters into drug policy – to begin the fairy tale analogy, the innocents are identified and we are also introduced to the possibility of a wicked ogre. The activities of the Quakers and the Quaker-led Society for the Suppression of the Opium Trade (SSOT) were key in this respect. Essentially, the moral argument ran that certain members of society suffered from "moral weakness" and could be easily corrupted into the luxurious use of opiates to gain inebriation. This marks an important turning point, because for the first time the unauthorised use of drugs moved from being seen as "normal" to being seen to represent a form of personal weakness, running counter to the prevailing morality (Barton, 2003; Berridge, 2005).

What we had by the time the 1800s came to an end was a hybrid model, in which the lay/commercial model was declining in influence and the pharmaceutical control/moral opposition model was growing in importance, as in reality there were elements of both still visible. This came to an abrupt end with the onset of World War I and a real concern as to the negative influence all forms of substance use could have on Britain's ability to win the War. Those concerns cemented the position of the Home Office and the justice agencies as key players in British drug policy. Central here is the Defence of the Realm Act (DORA), which allowed wartime leaders to intervene in all manner of areas of state and social life. Essentially, DORA was a form of martial law that allowed the state to pass laws without recourse to full parliamentary channels. Initially, Mott and Bean (1998) argue, a series of moral panics over the "contaminating effect" of prostitutes and the recreational use of cocaine by British and Canadian troops was at the heart of the legislative change. In July 1916, DORA 40B, by which the British State made its first big inroads into defining and controlling "harmful" substances, came into force.

South (1997, p. 937) notes that "a significant step had been taken", because unauthorised supply and all unauthorised possession were criminalised. In turn, this moved the Home Office to the centre stage in terms of government policy on substance use and misuse. Edwards (1981) posits that the passing of the 1920 Dangerous Drugs Act marks the birth of our contemporary system, as from 1920 onwards possession of all opiate- and cocaine-based products without authorisation or medical prescription became proscribed, with heavy legal penalties and social disapproval for those infringing the regulations.

As a consequence, the position of the medical profession became problematic and this ultimately led to the formation of the Rolleston Committee in 1925. In 1926, Rolleston found in favour of the retention of significant medical input into the "problem" of substance misuse. Key amongst the Committee's findings was the argument that the prescribing of opiates should be seen as a legitimate medical treatment, which should therefore remove the threat of prosecution from doctors prescribing maintenance doses. By acknowledging the right to prescribe, Rolleston established that addiction and substance misuse were medical problems to be addressed by doctors, not police officers.

By virtue of its findings, Rolleston created a "British system" (Berridge, 2005), whereby drug dependent users who were prepared to play the "sick role" were able to receive a regular supply of heroin or morphine in order to maintain or gradually reduce their use. The legacy of Rolleston was to create a dual approach to substance use and misuse. On the one hand, the police retained the power to prosecute unauthorised use, supply and possession, and thus to criminalise drug users not authorised by the medical profession. On the other hand, the medical profession retained the right to diagnose, define and treat addiction. In this way, a dual approach developed, with substance misusers being able to be defined as criminal or sick, depending on which arm of the British system they came in touch with.

Paralleling this was a shift in the moral and cultural view of drug taking. By the 1920s, the public's reaction to drug use had shifted considerably and the British public were no longer seeing drug taking as "normal". The death of actress Billie Carleton in 1919 and dance instructor Freda Kempton in 1922 received major publicity in the emergent tabloid press, with both females being seen as "victims" of drug dealers (Berridge, 2005). This fascination highlighted that the public were making distinctions between innocent victims of "the drug scourge" and the "ogres" who sold and distributed drugs. It is also worth noting that the media emphasised the involvement of "outsiders" and "foreigners" in the supply of these newly dangerous substances. Mott and Bean (1998, p. 40), for example, point to extensive media coverage of the trials of Edgar Manning, a Jamaican, and Brilliant Chang, a Chinese, for their involvement in trafficking cocaine.

This dual vision of drug users and drug use has created a system in which illicit drug use can be both medicalised and criminalised. Whilst the actual complexity of the situation surrounding illicit drug use is recognised by the professionals working in either field, the same cannot be said of the tabloids, which seemingly adopt a simplistic vision of drug use and drug users. The media perceive drug use through what are essentially morality-based, polar-opposite viewpoints, seeing drug users either as ill, adopting the role of a patient and therefore deserving of treatment and sympathy, or as bad, unrepentant hedonists who are often supplying and encouraging others to take drugs and are therefore deserving of our rage and contempt. In short, this dichotomous view encourages us to conceive of illicit drug users as either corrupted innocents or hedonistic ogres. Is the reality of illicit drug use in modern Britain as simplistic and easily understood as the morality-based division between corrupted innocent and hedonistic ogre suggests? In order to address this, we need to move toward examining the actual extent of illicit drug use.

Illicit drug use in contemporary England and Wales

The call for a more truthful approach to illicit drug use is at the core of this work, which requires openness about the limitations of our arguments. One such limitation is the veracity of any claims made in terms of numbers of users. The illicit and therefore hidden nature of drug taking means that we are unable to measure accurately the extent

126

The Media and Illicit Drug Use

and nature of use and are reliant on (well informed) best guesses, which are produced by amalgamating self-report surveys such as the *British Crime Survey* and examining seizure data from Customs and Revenue and the Police. With that in mind, the following section draws on data produced by the Home Office to paint a picture of illicit drug use in England and Wales (Chivite-Matthews et al., 2005).

At first glance, the rate of illicit drug use in England and Wales appears high – 35.6% of the population (about 11 million people) aged 16-59 claim to have used an illicit substance in their lifetime. However, what is termed "lifetime use" is probably not the best indicator of the overall picture. This is because lifetime use can refer to one episode of use – such as Bill Clinton's admission that he smoked, but did not inhale. Looking at time-specific measurements, 12.3% of the population aged 16-59 (about 4 million people) have used an illicit drug in the last year and 7.5% of the population (2 million people) have used an illicit drug in the last month.

However, these figures are perhaps misleading. If we factor age into the analysis, the numbers of users and frequency of use changes and arguably provides us with the ability to produce a picture of an identikit illicit drug user in contemporary Britain that is far removed from the innocents or ogres portrayed by the media. When we examine the figures for people aged 16-24, the picture changes: 46.6% of people aged 16-24 admit to lifetime use; 27.8% have used drugs in the last year; and 17.3% in the last month. Overwhelmingly, the drug of choice for this group of the population is cannabis, with just short of one in four (24.8%) 16-24 year-olds having used it in the last year. Behind cannabis comes ecstasy (5.3%), cocaine (4.9%), amyl nitrate (4.4%), and amphetamines (4%). Only 0.4% (25,000) of people aged 16-24 had used opiates in the last year. Moreover, the age group where illicit drug use is most prevalent is the 20-24 age range; they are twice as likely to use an illicit substance as the rest of the population. Interestingly, these trends have stayed remarkably stable since 1996.

We can also begin to look at the socio-demographics of illicit drug users, in order to build our picture. Users are overwhelmingly male, with a ratio of male to female users approaching 4:1. They are also likely to be single, unemployed, have an income of between £5,000 and £10,000 per annum, live in a privately rented flat and be educated to 'A' level standard. When employed, they have either skilled or semi-skilled occupations. They are more likely to visit clubs and pubs than their peers who do not use illicit drugs. This pattern is summarised by the Home Office researchers:

> ... being young ... being male, visiting nightclubs, not being married ... frequenting a pub or wine bar three times a week or more, living in a flat/maisonette or terraced house and living in a household with no children or being a single adult with children. (Chivite-Matthews et al., 2005, p. 59).

What of the argument that any illicit drug use will serve as a gateway into drug use that moves beyond recreational and into problematic use? If that were the case, we could expect high numbers of people both in receipt of or waiting for treatment. Department of Health figures for 2004/05 show that 160,050 drug users are currently in treatment, of whom 54% were retained for longer than 12 weeks (UK Department of Health, 2005). The majority of those were being treated for opiate addiction tended to be older (Bennett & Holloway, 2005) than those admitting to high levels of use in the general population.

Finally, what do we know about the drug market? If the media-inspired picture of hedonistic, spell-casting ogres waiting to ensnare innocents is correct, then we would expect to see a supply-led market, in which suppliers need to promote their product in order to encourage new entrants into the market (Fuller, 1990). Research indicates that the opposite is true, with the illicit drug market being demand-driven. Parker et al. (1998) offer a fascinating insight into the journeys that led to young people taking drugs. Most first take drugs in relaxed social situations with friends and often these drugs are "free", in as much as, if person A has drugs, then they will often share them with person B, and vice versa. What is equally clear from this research is that the line between "dealer" and "user" (or, in our case, ogre and innocent) is incredibly blurred. Finally, Parker and his colleagues found that drug taking opportunities were as likely to be rejected as they were to be accepted. This seemingly points to a coherent and objective decision being taken by the informed, knowledgeable and, importantly, *consenting* drug user, far removed from pressure or coercion by a "seedy pusher" selling a substance to a naive and ill-informed innocent.

Overall, then, what are we to make of illicit drug use in early twenty-first century Britain? Bearing in mind the caveats mentioned at the start of this section about the accuracy of the measurements, it is possible to suggest that in England and Wales:

- Somewhere in the region of 11 million people – more than a third of the adult population – have used an illicit drug at least once;

- Close to half of all people aged 16–24 have used an illicit drug at least once;

- Over a million people aged 16-24 have used an illicit drug this month;

- Cannabis is overwhelmingly the most popular drug, with the "hard" drugs of heroin and cocaine falling a long way behind;

- The use and likelihood of use of an illicit drug diminishes with age;

- There are somewhere in the region of 250,000 problematic illicit drug users in England and Wales, with about 160,000 of those in some form of treatment;

- The majority of illicit drug users do so recreationally or experimentally.

How can we make sense of a situation in which, statistically at least, over a third of all adults have tried an illicit drug at least once and approaching 50% of young people admit to some form of illicit drug use, but in which the media seem keen on continuing the "ogre/innocent" dichotomy? How are we to reconcile reportage with reality? Where do we look to find the real world ogres?

Are they amongst the 11 million users? Even given what we know about demographics and drug use, it is possible to posit that one in three male police officers, judges, politicians, doctors, teachers, university lecturers, journalists and so on will have used an illicit substance at least once – are they all innocents? Indeed, the recent bout of confessions from members of the New Labour Cabinet emphasises the widespread, youthful use of cannabis amongst many holders of high office (*The Times*, 2007, July 19).

At the same time, we know that, at the user level of the illicit drug market, the distinction between dealer and user is blurred, with many users "dealing" to ensure their own supply or simply procuring drugs for their friends. Thus, it is probable that many recreational users, however infrequently they have used drugs, have at one time or another become a dealer in the eyes of the law, because they have supplied drugs to another person – are they all ogres?

Finally, it is clear that there are two distinct types of illicit drug user: the majority, who do so infrequently and unproblematically; and the minority, for whom illicit drug use becomes the source of a number of related social, medical and criminal problems – is it the case that the former group are the innocents and the latter group the ogres?

If we cannot adequately answer these questions, then the media's insistence on portraying drug use in the oppositional terms of ogre and innocent becomes questionable. I wish to continue by examining two aspects of illicit drug use that are occurring in Britain and which are working against each other: one is the manner in which the media choose to see illicit drug use as a moral (and thus ultimately criminal) problem and the resulting impact this has on the way in which illicit drug use is reported; and the other relates to ongoing cultural shifts, which are rapidly creating a situation in which we need a major and open debate about our attitudes and policy responses to illicit drug use. It is the former that exercises the media, and in turn limits our ability to "Get Real" (UK Home Office, Drug Prevention Advisory Service, 2001) in discussing illicit drug use and illicit drug policy. It is to these two aspects that this paper now turns its attention.

The media and the portrayal of illicit drug use

In policy terms, illicit drug use can be defined as a criminal problem or a medical problem, or more frequently in twenty-first century Britain as a combination of both (Barton, 1999). However, the media almost always chooses to see illicit drug use as a moral/criminal problem first, with any reference to treatment coming in the guise of a visit to "rehab" or "a clinic". Moreover, whilst research seems to indicate that most drug use is experimental and infrequent, media attention is biased toward the minority of users whose use has become problematic. Although this is a distortion of reality, it seems to have an effect on the public and policymakers (Blackman, 2004).

Above, we have seen that the tabloid press often use lurid headlines and images in their portrayal of illicit drug use. Pete Doherty seems to be the current scapegoat of the tabloids, but at different times the examples used could have been Craig Charles, Michael Barrymore, Brian Harvey, or even Sir Paul McCartney, who was arrested, imprisoned and then deported from Japan in 1980 for attempting to import 219 grams (7.7 ounces) of cannabis; this was his fourth prosecution for illicit drug possession and his second for importation (Wasserman, 1980, July). Regardless of the subject, the reporting perpetuates the fairy tale distinction between ogre and innocent. Thus, in terms of facilitating a much-needed discussion on where we take illicit drug policy in the twenty-first century, the manner in which the media "deal with" illicit drugs becomes of paramount importance.

For example, Levi (2006, p. 1038), in discussing the influence of the media in crime reporting, suggests that:

the media shapes crime discourses and may well influence public perceptions of harmfulness and of what the "law and order problem" consists of, with consequent effects on:

- enforcement resources (including policing powers);
- the decision making of juries and other tribunals ....

The media can also directly cause us to rethink policy, as well as "... illuminate the politics of representation of some social groups and try to account for this" (Levi, p. 1039). Reiner (2002, pp. 402-404) argues that, when the media report on crime, they represent "hegemony in action", which occurs as a result of:

1. The conservative nature of the press, which leads to the middle of the road majority options becoming the "common sense" view;

2. The need for stories to be newsworthy, which explains the over-representation of lurid crimes; and

3. The structural determinants of news making, which allows criminal justice organisations to become the primary definers of crime news.

This echoes the work of Felson (2002, p. 2), who suggests that the media indulges in "horror-distortion sequences" and, as a result, there are "ten fallacies" about crime which the media perpetuates, with the result that "... public misinformation grows, with new stories building on public acceptance of past misconceptions. So it is no accident that crime becomes distorted in the public mind". This is arguably the case with the British press and the reporting of illicit drug use.

Consumption, culture and the new morality

Looking at the cultural aspect of drug use, it is difficult to disagree with Courtwright (2001, p. 96), who argues that it is impossible to disentangle the use of psychotropic substances and culture. Clearly, contemporary culture in Britain is fluid at present (Blackman, 2004) and I wish to argue that we are seeing the development of a culture which sees the recreational use of certain proscribed substances as being in some instances "normal", or at least to be *expected* in certain situations and amongst certain social groups, and therefore of no great consequence. I would suggest that, amongst a significant minority of the young and a lesser minority of the general population, the recreational use of illicit drugs has ceased to become the subject of a moral dilemma and is rapidly moving away from even being viewed as "wrong".

Instead, illicit drug use has become what Felson (2002) has termed a "crime of everyday life". By that, it is meant that people who would otherwise be described as members of the law-abiding majority and see themselves as respectable citizens have no moral problem in breaking the drug laws, and view their actions as an acceptable cultural activity rather than a serious crime. Thus, illicit drug taking for some of the population in contemporary Britain has become akin to other "... types of crime [that] fall into the grey zone of morality" (Karstedt & Farrall 2006, p. 1011), which include driving through red traffic lights, making fraudulent insurance claims, and undertaking or paying for work done in the black economy. Karstedt and Farrall (2006) expand on this in terms of the moral economy of day-to-day living and make some interesting claims with regard to crimes of everyday life. In particular, they see activity that falls into the grey zone of morality as being, not the sole preserve of individual morality, but rather as indicative of the overall moral state of society.

They suggest that our current morality is linked to the promotion of consumerism and that neo-liberal economic policies have transformed how we conceive individuals and our relationship with the state and civil society, with an accompanying effect on the shape of our shared morality. Specifically, these changes encourage:

1. Self-advancement, by seeing the world as entrepreneurial and thus full of negotiable risks;

2. Consumerism, declared to be sovereign in a deregulated and risk-heavy market place, which places all relationships into consumer-based ones; and

3. Consumerism, leading to a reshaping of the relationship between individuals, the state, the law and morality, thus shifting definitions of fair, just, legitimate and moral towards consumer- and market-led perceptions.

In essence, contemporary culture revolves around choice, freedom to consume and the ability to make calculated "life-style" choices, which are furnished and encouraged by a largely unregulated market.

For some of the population, taking and sharing (and thus in legal terms dealing in) illicit drugs becomes just another consumption choice, which fits with a market-led, consumer-focused, collective morality (Van Ree, 2002). Drug use falls into the grey zone of morality, in which an activity becomes placed on a continuum from illegal to shady. However, the law lacks either legitimacy or enforceability in the eyes of the transgressors and their peer group. As Karstedt and Farrall (2006, p. 1030) note,

"Citizens discuss justifications and techniques of committing crimes of everyday life with considerable ease, thus creating a moral climate which encourages such types of behaviour." As a result, for a significant minority of the population, taking some types of illicit drugs becomes devoid of questions about right and wrong and makes the tabloids' polar views between ogres and innocents redundant.

Conclusion

To summarise, British drug policy has developed as a result of two forces: the need of the medical profession to "own" certain substances and successive shifts in public morality, which have seen the use of substances change from normal and accepted to deviant and wrong. The British Model allowed drug use to be both criminalised and medicalised, but increasingly these two approaches have become merged, albeit with a criminal justice bias. This paper has also argued that, in today's Britain, a significant minority of the population has ceased to see the use of illicit drugs as amoral and that drug use has become a crime of everyday life, in much the same way as jumping red lights, making fraudulent insurance claims or paying cash in hand for work to avoid tax. Drug use is now part of the everyday experiences of over a third of adults aged between 16 and 60 and the majority of illicit drug users do so unproblematically and simply "grow out of it" as they get older. Despite this, media representations of illicit drug use continue to concentrate on problematic use and atypical examples, due to the "horror–distortion process" identified by Felson (2002).

As a result, public perceptions of drug use become skewed by atypical examples, which do not reflect the lived reality or experience of most illicit drug users. The drug-related stories the public are fed by the media are little more than fairy tale-like morality stories, which divide drug users into hedonistic ogres or naive innocents and which imply seduction, contamination via spell-casting, and happy endings in which redemption and "saving" come as a result either of the love and support of an innocent or interventions by quasi-medical clinics. Whilst this may sell newspapers, such an approach does little to pave the way for a much-needed debate as to the future direction of British drug policy in an era in which public morality and concern seem to be moving against current policy and law. Until we tire of such stories, the chances of politicians making significant policy changes to match the reality of the drug milieu in the twenty-first century seem as unlikely as Beauty not saving the Beast.

References

Barton, A. (1999). Sentenced to treatment?: Criminal justice orders and the health service. *Critical Social Policy, 19,* 463-483.

Barton, A. (2003). *Illicit drugs: Use and control.* London: Routledge.

Bennett, T., & Holloway, K. (2005). *Understanding drugs, alcohol and crime.* Maidenhead: Open University Press.

Berridge, V. (2005). The 'British System' and its history: Myth and reality. In J. Strang & M. Gossop, M. (Eds.), *Heroin addiction and the British system: Vol. 1. Origins and evolution* (pp. 7-16). London: Routledge.

Blackman, S. J. (2004). *Chilling out: The cultural politics of substance consumption, youth and drug policy.* Maidenhead: Open University Press.

Chivite-Matthews, N., Richardson, A., O'Shea, J., Becker, J., Owen, N., Roe, S., & Condon, J. (2005). *Drug misuse declared: Findings from the 2003/04 British Crime Survey: England and Wales.* London: Home Office, Research, Development and Statistics Directorate.

Coleman, V. (1985). *The story of medicine.* London: Hale.

Courtwright, D. T. (2001). *Forces of habit: Drugs and the making of the modern world.* Cambridge, MA: Harvard University Press.

Daily Star. (2006, September 11). Sick Pete's blood lust.

Dangerous Drugs Act: 10 & 11 Geo. 5, Chapter 46. (1920). London: H.M.S.O.

Defence of the Realm Act: 4 & 5 Geo. 5, Chapter 29 (1914). London: King's Printer of Acts of Parliament.

Edwards, G. (1981). The background. In G. Edwards & C. Busch (Eds.), *Drug problems in Britain: A review of ten years.* London: Academic Press.

Felson, M. (2002). *Crime and everyday life.* (3rd ed.). Thousand Oaks, CA: Sage. (Original ed. published, 1994).

Fuller, N. (1990). *Fundamental economics.* (2nd ed.). Eastham: Tudor. (Original ed. published 1987).

Hooker , R. (1996). *The Opium Wars.* Retrieved March 26, 2008, from:

http://www.wsu.edu:8080/~dee/CHING/OPIUM.H TM.

Karstedt, S., & Farrall, S. (2006). The moral economy of everyday crime: Markets, consumers and citizens. *The British Journal of Criminology, 46* (6), 1011–1036.

Levi, M. (2006). The media construction of financial white-collar crimes. *The British Journal of Criminology, 46* (6), 1037–1057.

Mott, J., & Bean, P. (1998). The development of drug control in Britain. In R. Coomber (Ed.), *The control of drug and drug users: Reason or reaction?* (pp. 31-48). Amsterdam: Harwood Academic.

Parker, H., Aldridge, J., & Measham, F. (1998). *Illegal leisure: The normalization of adolescent recreational drug use.* London: Routledge.

Reiner, R. (2002). Media made criminality: The representation of crime in the mass media. In M. Maguire, R. Morgan, & R. Reiner, (Eds.), *The Oxford handbook of criminology* (3rd ed., pp. 376-414). Oxford: Oxford University Press. (Original ed. published 1994).

Rolleston, H. (1926). *Report of the Departmental Committee on Morphine and Heroin Addiction.* London: H.M.S.O.

SoFeminine co.uk. (2006, March 17). Kate Moss to 'rescue' Pete Doherty from drugs hell. Retrieved March 26, 2008, from: http://www.sofeminine.co.uk/w/star/n116040/news / Kate–Moss-to-Rescue–Pete-Doherty-from-Drugs - Hell.html.

South, N. (1997). Drugs: Use, crime and control. In M. Maguire, R. Morgan, & R. Reiner, (Eds.), *The Oxford handbook of criminology* (2nd ed., pp. 925-960). Oxford: Oxford University Press. (Original ed. published, 1994).

The Sun. (2006, June 30). Kate: My lines for Doherty.

The Times. (2007, July 19). Seven Cabinet members admit taking cannabis.

UK Department of Health. (2005). *United Kingdom drug situation: Annual report to the European Monitoring Centre for Drugs and Drug Addiction (EMCDDA), 2005.* Liverpool : UK Focal Point on Drugs.

UK Home Office. Drug Prevention Advisory Service. (2001). *Let's get real: Communicating with the public about drugs*. London: Author.

Van Ree, E. (2002). Drugs, the democratic civilising process and the consumer society. *The International Journal of Drug Policy, 13* (5), 349–353.

Wasserman, H. (1980, July). Paul's pot-bust shocker makes him a jailhouse rocker [Electronic version]. *High Times*. Retrieved November 14, 2006, from:

www.taima.org/en/hemplib3.htm#mccartney

"SLEEPWALKING" INTO AN ORWELLIAN NIGHTMARE: SURVEILLANCE, POLICING AND CONTROL IN THE 21ST CENTURY

John Harrison

Introduction

The key focus of this paper is to explore what is described by some as the increasing prevalence of surveillance within contemporary society in the United Kingdom. While the technological advances that lead to surveillance are available throughout Western industrialised societies, it is in the UK and possibly the USA that they are utilised most extensively. A significant feature of this increase in surveillance is the gradual acceptance that this is simply a rational development of technological advances that have become a part of everyday life, predicated on a belief that the security of society is best served by this type of activity. While critics of surveillance point to Human Rights and Civil Liberties, arguing that this is a breach of individual privacy, proponents claim this response to rising crime and increases in terrorist activity is justified and, in any event, "if you have nothing to hide, why worry".

While my argument draws on the novels of George Orwell, I do not suggest that his apparently intuitive writing has been proved to be accurate; rather, the goal is to demonstrate the extent to which we have allowed increased levels of surveillance to become an integral feature of our daily activities, without noticing any significant level of intrusion into our lives. The second theme highlighted here is how, while this surveillance is allegedly focused on identifying and deterring those who threaten communities and protecting the security of neighbourhoods and the wider society, it is in fact monitoring the movements of everyone in society. Increasingly high levels of surveillance have become an accepted part of contemporary Western culture; not only in an acceptance that the majority of people going about their normal daily business will be captured on CCTV several hundred times a day, but also in the development of popular culture and entertainment, voyeuristic journalism and in the representation of political debate. Arguably, this has a wider bearing on criminal justice legislation, anti-terrorist legislation, responses to anti-social behaviour and on the development of a wide range of criminal justice legislation, policy and practice. In addition, these heightened levels of surveillance are becoming increasingly evident in relation to welfare, health, education and community life.

In this paper, "Orwellian Nightmare" refers to George Orwell's novel *Nineteen Eighty-Four*, written in 1949, and to the comments in an interview published in *The Times* newspaper in 2004 (and quoted in *Statewatch News online*) by the Information Commissioner, Richard Thomas, that Britain was "sleepwalking into a surveillance society". He was quoted as saying:

> My anxiety is that we don't sleepwalk into a surveillance society where much more information is collected about people, accessible to far more people, shared across many more boundaries, than British society would feel comfortable with ....
>
> Some of my counterparts in Eastern Europe, in Spain, have experienced in the last century what can happen when government gets too powerful and has too much information on citizens. When everyone knows everything about everybody else and the Government has got massive files, whether manual or computerised ....

I don't think people have woken up to what lies behind this. It enables the Government of the day to build up quite a comprehensive picture about many of your activities. My job is to make sure no more information is collected than necessary for any particular purpose.

(http://www.statewatch.org/news/2004/aug/08uk-info-commissioner.htm)

The argument presented in this chapter, then, is that the cultural acceptance of everyday surveillance is reducing the awareness of the general population to the fact that society is becoming increasingly controlled and monitored; that we acquiesce in the increased accumulation of data about our daily lives and personal actions and that in the main we are compliant in this increased loss of privacy. The suggestion is that we have become less aware of the intrusiveness of some state legislation and practices and to some extent have been seduced by the belief that, in order to maintain the security of the UK, both internally and externally, we need to give up certain rights to ensure that we know what the "bad guys" are doing. One of the key concerns here is the question of who decides who the "bad guys" are and how we identify them.

Orwell's dystopian novel was not initially seen to be of any significance when it was first published. It was commonly viewed as a response to totalitarianism, which was seen to be the consequence of some of the revolutionary uprisings of the early 20th century. The book's origins are often traced to the rise of a "Stalinist" state in the Soviet region and in the Spanish Civil War, in which Orwell fought. A common interpretation of this novel is that it represents support for democratic socialism over totalitarianism; the increased surveillance described is a demonstration of the perils of allowing the state to become totally controlling in its power. It is not my intention to provide a summary of the novel, but to discuss the impact that the book ultimately had on Western culture, particularly in the context of contemporary British society. It is, however, interesting to note that much of the technological "fiction" that Orwell described has become a reality in 21st century Britain. CCTV can monitor the streets and the insides of buildings, and indeed we can observe the way that people live their lives in their own homes; this has become increasingly acceptable in the context of "entertainment" through reality television. For Orwell, surveillance involved individuals being watched in their own homes, neighbours spying on them and their families informing on them when they challenged the official line. In a more contemporary "entertainment" sense, we are able to watch the behaviour of particular social groups in television programmes like *Wife Swap*, while other programmes look at the problems presented by "problem children". For example, *Super Nanny* shows where families are going wrong in bringing up their children and guides them through steps to correct their "bad parenting" practices. While many watch this as a documentary about others and how they live, other viewers may well look on this as an educational programme on parenting skills! This use of the media to demonstrate the apparent inadequacies of some parents may well be a significant feature in the popular acceptance of the view that "parenting orders" are an appropriate response to youth offending and anti-social behaviour and have a place in crime and disorder legislation, such as the Anti-social Behaviour Act 2003.

In this cultural context, Orwell's work continues to influence contemporary discourse through media representations of "Room 101" and "Big Brother". Orwell describes "Room 101" as a place where those who resist the power of the state are ultimately taken to be confronted with the "worst fear they can imagine". The assumption is that the threat of being forced to confront these fears will imbue a level of control and compliance. In the case of Winston Smith (the key character in *Nineteen Eighty-Four*) this consists of being forced to go into Room 101 with a pack of rats, Smith's greatest fear. In contemporary popular culture *Room 101* (BBC TV and Radio) has become a place for "celebrities" to leave their pet hates. A more recent television phenomenon is *Big Brother* (Channel Four), where we see people living together in a house and having their every move monitored and watched and analysed by the audience. This use of entertainment is, as Presdee (2000) suggests, significantly problematic, as it encourages humiliation and compliance to a particular style of behaviour to achieve a maximum of public exposure. Perhaps not quite what Orwell implied, but nonetheless a significant intrusion into the world of "watching others".

It is not just in an entertainment context that we have seen a growing acceptance of surveillance. The Orwellian "Big Brother", an all-seeing, manipulative and ultimately all-powerful state, is increasingly seen as the norm in contemporary Britain in the case of criminal justice policy and practice. Social theorists and researchers have long argued that, in understanding society, we need to develop an understanding of human association (Simmel, 1950; cited in Hier & Greenberg, 2007); this understanding of social relationships allows us to identify and explain changes in behaviour, observe inappropriate behaviour and recognise those who are "out of place" in a specific environment. These aspects have become significant in the context of crime reduction and social control. There are many examples of how attempts to reduce crime have built on our willingness to watch others, with an increased emphasis on reporting to the relevant authorities those whose behaviour is unacceptable or inappropriate.

To take Neighbourhood Watch as an example; according to the Home Office's Crime Reduction website:

> Neighbourhood Watch is one of the biggest and most successful crime prevention initiatives ever. Behind it lies a simple idea, and a central value shared by millions of people around the country:
>
> > Everyone knows that the police are there to fight crime, but they need your help to do an effective job. Neighbourhood Watch (or Home Watch as it is known in some areas) is all about an active partnership with the police. Neighbourhood Watch schemes can
> >
> > - cut crime and the opportunities for crime;
> > - help and reassure those who live in the area;
> > - encourage neighbourliness and closer communities.
>
> (http://www.crimereduction.homeoffice.gov.uk/nbhwatch.htm)

Neighbourhood Watch, of course, relies heavily on individuals in local communities observing their neighbours, visitors and, perhaps crucially, "outsiders" to identify any behaviour that may be illegal or potentially criminal and advise their local police service. This is not unlike the theme identified by Orwell, when neighbours "spied" on their neighbours and reported inappropriate behaviour to the secret police. More recently, the fears of terrorist activity in Britain and the USA have fostered this surveillance culture in relation to specific social groups who are seen to be a threat; the identification of "problem groups" is discussed in greater depth later in the chapter. Increased use of the media to raise awareness of those we should be watching and the identification of appropriate behaviour have become central themes in contemporary society.

Surveillance and technology

This increase in surveillance is a theme identified in a report prepared for the Government's Information Commissioner (Surveillance Studies Network, 2006), which highlights the fact that:

> We live in a surveillance society. It is pointless to talk about surveillance society in the future tense. In all the rich countries of the world, everyday life is suffused with surveillance encounters, not merely from dawn to dusk, but 24/7. Some encounters obtrude into the routine, like when we get a ticket for running a red light when no one was around but the camera. But the majority are now just part of the fabric of daily life. Unremarkable.

It is remarkable that the significant level of routine surveillance taking place goes unnoticed for the most part; indeed it is questionable whether we even realise the amount of data being accumulated in relation to our daily activities.

The increased use of CCTV cameras means that our images may be captured several hundred times daily (Surveillance Studies Network, 2006), while supermarket checkouts gather data on our shopping habits, methods of payment and personal bank details. As the convenience of the move towards a "cashless society" becomes more widely accepted, so does the acceptance that such forms of data collection are not only necessary, but pose no threat to our security and well-being; in turn, we become more accepting of routine surveillance. This type of monitoring, of course, does not equal the images of the more sinister and totalitarian surveillance that Orwell highlights, but it reduces our scepticism about the involvement of the state in our daily lives. The level of surveillance envisaged in *A report on the surveillance society* (Surveillance Studies Network) gives the impression that increased surveillance is a contemporary concern enabled by technological advances. This, of course, is not the case, as various levels of surveillance can be observed throughout history. Lyon reminds us that "the rise in modern surveillance societies has everything to do with disappearing bodies" (2001; cited in Hier & Greenberg, 2007). Technological advances have significantly altered the way in which social relationships are conducted and "face-to-face" contact is no longer the preferred form of communication and identification. Increasingly, communication is via the internet, telephone, text messaging and other new technologies. This increases our reliance on passwords, PIN numbers and other remote forms of identification and leaves behind us an "electronic snail trail".

Foucault (1961/1998; 1975/1979) discusses the impact of technologies in the control of individuals, highlighting the use of the "panopticon", particularly in the context of prisons (1975/1979). This system of observing the prisoner and ensuring that prisoners knew that their every action was being observed was designed to impact on their behaviour. This is the justification in contemporary society for the increased use of CCTV and other surveillance activities: the fear that we are being observed prevents us from contravening formal or informal norms of acceptable behaviour. This institutional surveillance is evident in all areas of our social lives: welfare, health, education, the workplace and the criminal justice system. While it is only possible to highlight some examples in each of these areas of our lives, this should allow for a greater understanding of how we increasingly see surveillance as normal and acceptable in the 21st century.

Welfare

During the second half of the 20th century, the involvement of welfare agencies in the daily lives of families, individuals and children increased dramatically. Many would argue that the growth of the social work profession from the early 1970s was a response to the changing needs of a society that exhibited an array of social problems related to increased family breakdown, decline in communities and increased dependence on social welfare. True, this was a period when "social problems" of this nature became more acute, but it was also a period when traditional institutions of control, such as the family and the workplace, were able to exert less influence over a significant proportion of society.

As we neared the end of the 20th century, concerns about a growing underclass were raised (Murray, 1990; 1996) and highlighted by the media. This section of society could be clearly identified and there were common features indicating that certain communities were part of this "problematic" section of society: teenage pregnancy, fatherless families, unemployment and increasing levels of violence. The response was to increase welfare involvement, in the form of the New Deal, Sure Start, the Children's Fund and Connexions, amongst others. At face value, these programmes appear to be a response to the social exclusion that is a feature of the growing underclass; they all seek to reduce the dependency of individuals, families and communities on welfare support and encourage greater independence from the state. Their focus, however, is not only on those who are unemployed, lone parents or poorly educated, but also on those "at risk" of social exclusion. Social exclusion, of course, is a recurring theme in understanding contemporary crime and disorder, anti-social behaviour and violence; as such, the involvement of welfare agencies in whatever form can arguably be seen as increased surveillance of the "dangerous classes". This term, which had largely died out in the early 20th century (Morris, 1994), was now becoming increasingly synonymous with the underclass.

Health

Surveillance in the context of health is generally perceived as a positive feature of contemporary society. Regular health checks, regular reminders about healthy eating habits and sensible consumption of "bad" things like alcohol, tobacco, salts, sugars and fatty foods have all contributed to a "nation enjoying healthier and longer lives". There is, however, a focus on specific groups perceived to be most at risk of ill health, owing to poor diet, drinking and smoking. Many would suggest this focuses on the social groups who experience the greatest levels of poverty, are least likely to enjoy a healthy lifestyle and perhaps live in the least prosperous communities; those at greatest risk of social exclusion. The relationship between poverty and health was highlighted in the *Black Report* (Black, Morris, Smith & Townsend, 1982) and, while relative poverty may have been less in evidence in the 1990s, the underlying principles continue to be significant.

This increased level of surveillance is evident in the increase in legislation designed to reduce risk and improve the general health of the nation. In July 2007, the smoking ban in public places began in England, having been introduced previously in Scotland, Ireland and Wales, which effectively "criminalised" smoking. It could be argued that this is always likely to be the ultimate sanction to ensure compliance with "good advice". Healthy eating and childhood obesity could see similar restrictions being placed on children in specific situations. Concern about the availability of "unhealthy" foods in schools has seen increased legislation to control the use of vending machines and the sponsorship of schools by crisp manufacturers, soft drink suppliers and fast food chains. So, if "good advice" is ignored, there is always recourse to legislation to ensure compliance and enable a level of surveillance.

Education

It might be argued that surveillance in the context of education is ensuring that all those of compulsory school age attend regularly. To some extent, this was the role envisaged of education welfare officers when compulsory education was introduced at the end of the 19th century. This type of surveillance involved individual officers being aware of all children in their "patch" and enrolling them at school as soon as they were old enough. While this role has expanded today, this enforcement of compulsory education is still a significant part of their role at the beginning of the 21st century.

Education also allows for the surveillance of those families seen to be at "risk of social exclusion", a term that is a recurring theme of much of the "softer" debates on surveillance: for example, in relation to welfare-based strategies that enable professionals to monitor children, parenting, education and physical development. Frequently, these interventions are targeting those most likely to engage in "problem behaviour". These are the families that may have poor relationships, be lacking in parenting skills, have a history of poor educational attainment or indeed have a history of criminal activity.

Through the involvement of education staff, including teachers, school nurses and welfare officers, it is possible to monitor the families in relation to health, welfare and behaviour. Many in the education system would see this as demanding too much from them, but increasingly we see power passing to head teachers in relation to the control of parents. Under powers in the Education and Inspections Act 2006, head teachers can apply directly to the courts for parenting orders in the event of children presenting specific problems at school.

The workplace

Surveillance in the workplace has been a theme in debates about social control since the expansion of industrialisation in the 18th and 19th centuries. From a Marxist perspective, this involved the control of the working classes by the powerful minority who owned the means of production. In the 21st century, there is a view that traditional levels of control and relationship between "master and servant" are no longer applicable. Whether or not this is true is a matter for lengthy debate, not possible in the context of this discussion, but there is scope to consider the extent to which surveillance in the workplace remains significant.

The traditional systems of "clocking on and off" are less in evidence, as clocking machines no longer sit at the entrance of most workplaces. It is less likely that employees will stamp a time card as they arrive and leave the factory, shop or office. This is a change that has coincided with the decline in industrialisation and a move away from traditional working-class jobs in the coal mines, shipyards and manufacturing plants. Interestingly, today's clocking on and off may well be more important, but less evident, in the shape of covert surveillance of timekeeping practices.

Logging on and off computers, logging on to tills, and the switching on and off of security systems allow our working practices to be monitored. This does not simply involve checking when we arrive and leave the workplace, but allows for surveillance of the various activities we engage in throughout the working day. New computer technologies enable the monitoring of email activity, internet searches and the timing of interaction with customers, colleagues and others. It is rare that some use of computers is not present in the workplaces of the 21st century.

The criminal justice system

In discussing the origin of the prison, Foucault (1975/1979) discusses surveillance used to exercise punishment of the mind. The panopticon design of prisons attained this, as prisoners believed that they were constantly being watched. While the design of prisons may have changed, surveillance remains a feature of contemporary punishment; however, in a criminal justice context, surveillance is much more pervasive than simply being used as a punishment.

CCTV is increasingly being used to monitor the behaviour of individuals and groups; this involves everyone being captured regularly on CCTV, at an estimated several hundred times daily. From a criminal justice viewpoint, the evidence gathered can be used to identify offenders and to some extent to anticipate potentially criminal activity. The police's increasing use of a variety of surveillance techniques to monitor potential and known criminals extends beyond the use of CCTV; in the case of prolific offenders, it can involve the police watching known offenders overtly and covertly over extended periods of time. A recent initiative in North

Yorkshire involved the routine surveillance of serial offenders, preceded by a letter saying that they were being shadowed, whether they knew it or not (*Network News Monthly*, 2007). Tagging, and in some cases satellite tracking, of known offenders and those released early from custody is frequently used. Intelligence-led policing and crime analysis are also forms of surveillance, as is the storage of information about known offenders.

From first steps to steady sleepwalking

This growth of control institutions may not be new, having initially developed in the 19th century, owing to the increased need for the maintenance of order in the growing towns and cities. Clearly, some level of "watching out for people" has always been in evidence. This could be in a caring context or indeed in the context of looking out for those who may threaten our well-being or our stability; however, there has been a steady increase in formal controls over an extended period. The increase in professionalisation in all of these areas of social life has led to a greater involvement with all of these bodies, and there is a growing acceptance that this is appropriate and that there are significant numbers of people who would be unable to contribute to the well-being of society without high levels of support and control. Of course, this may reflect the organisational practices of contemporary society more than the totalitarianism suggested by Orwell; from a Weberian perspective, the change can be argued to be the result of "rationalised" progress towards efficient administration, following the technological revolution of the late 20th century.

The last years of the 20th century saw a significant increase in the "fear of crime". This has come about partly as a consequence of the politicisation of crime and disorder

(Brake & Hale, 1992) and partly as a consequence of the creation of "the other" as the focus of criminal justice policy and practice. Brake and Hale argue that it was only in the 1970s that law and order became a significant issue for political debate, following industrial decline in Britain and other Western capitalist states. The increased emphasis on the rights and responsibilities of individuals, some suggested, meant that there was no longer such a thing as society. Margaret Thatcher suggested as much in an interview with a popular woman's magazine (Keay, 1987). The main thrust of the argument was that a growing number of individuals perceived that they had a range of problems, but they expected the government to "sort it out" for them. This created a situation in which no responsibility for personal actions was evident and the blame for criminal behaviour, exclusion and lack of opportunity fell on to others. The growing numbers of young people excluded from the workplace was increasingly seen as a significant problem because they relied on state welfare, but also because the controls imposed by being in the workplace, training or in education were no longer evident. Increasingly, their behaviour was interpreted as problematic, and by the early 1990s there were large groups identified as a welfare-dependent "underclass" (Murray, 1990). Typically, this included teenage mothers living away from the fathers of their children and reliant on state benefits, and young men who rejected the formal workplace, preferring to rely on a range of illegal activities to support themselves and engaging in increased levels of violent behaviour.

This has been extended to include truants, young people not in education, training or employment, and rough sleepers. It was this underclass and all others who were on the margins of society that became the focus for the Labour government elected in 1997; Tony Blair, the

Prime Minister, highlighted the social inclusion of all members of society as a priority for the new Government. The Social Exclusion Unit, established in 1997, has focused on many of these groups as being in need of increased policy interventions and support. In addressing their needs, however, there has been an increase in the surveillance of the communities in which they live. Although I suggested earlier that all are subject to constant surveillance, some groups are much more likely to be focused on than others; resources (or lack of resources) mean that some level of targeting or prioritising is always going to be necessary in maintaining order and control in society.

Identifying the 'deviant'

Although to some extent we all make use of stereotypes when meeting new people or engaging in new situations, in a crime prevention or crime reduction context we can be seen to make considerable use of such stereotypes. Many of the contemporary "folk devils and moral panics" (Cohen, 1973; 2002) are based around stereotypical images. We have seen an increased use of stereotypes in relation to young people as a source of problems of disorder and criminal behaviour; "hoodies", "chavs", gangs and certain ethnic groups have all received widespread media attention. This contributes to our understanding of those who pose a threat to stability and informs decision making when targeting potential problems. The reality is that there is a need to target resources and to identify those concerns that are prominent with the public. As it is impossible to address all individual concerns, those fears that receive the greatest attention have to be promoted most vehemently. These are frequently developed as a consequence of media representations, which in turn feed the fear of crime. For example, as faith-based terrorism has become a significant concern for most Western democracies, so the stereotypical *jihad* terrorist was born.

No longer are we concerned about strangers with Irish accents, bent on creating fear and terror on mainland Britain; this threat is no longer so significant! Following 9/11 and 7/7, our focus is on Asians and Muslims; there is an assumption that all of those who oppose Western capitalism are from such communities. This is exacerbated by the fact that those "found guilty" of involvement in the terrorism of the early 21st century are from these communities. This is not to suggest that members of these groups are any more likely to be involved in terrorism, or indeed in any other form of criminal behaviour; but from the perspective of surveillance, control and policing, it is clear that we create our contemporary "folk devils", we exploit the fear of the public, and we encourage ever more surveillance to minimise the risk to stability and security. This has allowed for an increased acceptance that emails, mobile phone calls, texts and traditional phone calls should be monitored, not just in those circumstances when national security is threatened, but on a daily basis for those seen to pose a risk. There is a growing belief that, if you have "done nothing wrong, then you have nothing to fear".

Increasingly, banks, government departments and health services hold data about us all; more sophisticated and more extensive databases will emerge in the future and the routine sharing of information is likely to increase. There is an ongoing debate about the need to introduce new forms of proof to confirm our identity, and ID cards holding a variety of information about us have been seen as a significant response to the fear of the "other" and those who steal identities. These, however, are only a few examples of the increased reliance on new technologies to monitor individuals and respond to rising levels of crime. Advances in genetic research have enabled the police to "solve crimes" using DNA samples left at crime scenes, by matching these to samples held on the DNA database.

Current legislation allows the police to take a sample and retain the DNA of anyone arrested for an indictable offence, even if they are subsequently found to be not guilty. The UK database is currently the largest in the Western world, with an estimated 24,000 children having their details stored, according to *The Independent* (2006). Recent debates have suggested that all UK citizens should have their DNA stored, to eliminate accusations of inequality and ensure that guilty individuals who could be convicted using DNA samples do not go free (*The Guardian*, 2007). Of course, DNA storage may have led to the police solving many unsolved serious crimes, such as murder, rape and serious sexual assaults. There is little doubt that these technologies have been beneficial in this context, but there is concern that the acceptance of a surveillance society will lead to even more people having their DNA samples stored.

Conclusion

The impact of surveillance means that we are never sure when we are being watched, we do not know how our "private lives" are being observed and indeed we do not know when and how any data held on us will be used. This increase in surveillance has become both culturally acceptable and routinely accepted as a means of increasing security and reducing fear of crime. We may still enjoy freedoms that Orwell suggested could disappear in a truly totalitarian state, but we are sacrificing, often unwittingly, ever more of our freedoms and rights. Is this a dream and are we sleepwalking to an Orwellian Nightmare? The argument in this chapter has been to emphasise the growing acceptance of surveillance as an everyday feature in contemporary society. This is partly attributable to an increase in the development of surveillance technology, such as CCTV, mobile phones, tagging systems and satellite tracking. In addition, we have seen the concept of watching others become a culturally acceptable activity, based on entertainment, reality TV and media intrusion into everyday activities. A wide range of social policy initiatives have contributed to the monitoring of "risky" behaviour and, in an increasing number of examples, have led to increased legislation and the criminalisation of some behaviour.

This increase in surveillance goes unchallenged by many, and is indeed frequently supported, as we become concerned about threats from outsiders, those who fail to make a significant contribution to community life and those who choose to rely on criminal activity to survive. Fear of crime, fear of "the other" and fear of those who are socially excluded has allowed surveillance to become a normal part of our daily lives, accepted because it increases security, and going unchallenged because we fear the strangers that infiltrate our stable communities and we are seduced by the arguments that risk and danger are all around and that constant vigilance will bring about a safer society. This then brings about a state of contentment when we believe we are being watched, allowing us to drift into a surveillance society in a dreamlike state.

References: Printed Sources

Anti-social Behaviour Act: Elizabeth II, 2003, Chapter 38.

    (2003). London: Stationery Office.

"Sleepwalking" into an Orwellian Nightmare

Black, D., Morris, J. N., Smith, C., & Townsend, P. (1982). *Inequalities in health: The Black Report* (P. Townsend & N. Davidson, Eds.). (New ed.). Harmondsworth: Penguin. (Originally published 1980).

Brake, M., & Hale, C. (1992). *Public order and private lives: The politics of law and order.* London: Routledge.

Cohen, S. (2002). *Folk devils and moral panics: The creation of the Mods and Rockers.* (3rd ed.). London: Routledge. (Originally published 1972).

Cohen, S. (1973). *Folk devils and moral panics: The creation of the Mods and Rockers.* (New ed.). St Albans: Paladin. (Originally published 1972).

Education and Inspections Act: Elizabeth II, 2006, Chapter 40. (2006). London: Stationery Office.

Foucault, M. (1979). *Discipline and punish: The birth of the prison* (A. Sheridan, Trans.). (New ed.). New York: Vintage Books. (Original work published 1975).

Foucault, M. (1998). *Madness and civilization: A history of insanity in the age of reason* (R. Howard, Trans.). (New ed.) New York: Vintage Books. (Original work published 1961).

Hier, S. P., & Greenberg, J. (2007) *The surveillance studies reader.* Maidenhead: Open University Press.

Keay, D. (1987, October 31). Aids, education and the year 2000. *Woman's Own*, 8-10.

Morris, L. (1994). *Dangerous classes: The underclass and social citizenship*. London: Routledge.

Murray, C. (1990). *The emerging British underclass*. London: IEA Health and Welfare Unit.

Murray, C. (1996). *Charles Murray and the underclass: The developing debate*. London: IEA Health and Welfare Unit, in association with the *Sunday Times*.

Orwell, G. (1949). *Nineteen eighty-four*. London: Secker & Warburg.

Presdee, M. (2000). *Cultural criminology and the carnival of crime*. London: Routledge.

References: Internet Sources

The Guardian. (2007, September 5). Judge wants everyone in UK on DNA database, by J. Orr and agencies. Retrieved May 23, 2008, from: http://www.guardian.co.uk/uk/2007/sep/05/human rights.ukcrime

Home Office (2007). *Welcome to Neighbourhood Watch*. Retrieved May 23, 2008, from:

"Sleepwalking" into an Orwellian Nightmare http://www.crimereduction.homeoffice.gov.uk/nbhw atch.htm

The Independent. (2006, April 14). More Britons have DNA held by police than rest of world, by N. Morris. Retrieved May 23, 2008, from: http://www.independent.co.uk/news/uk/crime/mor e-britons-have-dna-held-by-police-than-rest-of-world-474078.html

Network News Monthly. (2007, October). Shadow boxes in the criminals. Retrieved May 23, 2008, from: http://www.community-safety.net/affiliates/downld-oct07/Shadow-Boxes-in-Criminals-Oct07.pdf

Statewatch News online. (2004, August). Sleepwalking into a surveillance society? Retrieved May 23, 2008, from: http://www.statewatch.org/news/2004/aug/08uk-info-commissioner.htm

Surveillance Studies Network. (2006, September). *A report on the surveillance society, for the Information Commissioner: Full report.* Retrieved May 23, 2008, from: http://www.ico.gov.uk/upload/documents/library/ data_protection/practical_application/surveillance_so ciety_full_report_2006.pdf

MANHATTAN MASQUERADE: SEXUALITY AND SPECTACLE IN THE WORLD OF QUENTIN CRISP

Mark J. Bendall

Introduction

During a Calvin Klein commercial for a unisex perfume, *CKOne*, Quentin Crisp, frail, nearly ninety, dwarfed by the young models gambling about him, wondered what it all meant (Q. Crisp, personal communication, June 1998). This chapter asks the same question about him: what did he mean to do and to be as he performed his masquerade? What did he mean to those who came across him? It interrogates the dissonance between what he said and what he was, the contradictions that ran through the mix of revelation and self-revulsion he appeared to represent. How does one understand his paradoxical desire for queer display on the one hand, yet his distance from, even damning of, that identity on the other? The successful manipulation and marketing of his sexuality as a profession implied a certain proud empowerment; yet his assertion that such sexuality is "unreal" indicated internalisation of prejudice. It is partly because of the stigmatisation of his own identity that Crisp, sometimes considered a camp icon, counts amongst his fiercest critics those within gay "communities".

These issues will be developed with reference to a series of interlocking factors. Crisp's parade of camp will be explored; his use of language, of code, of wit as weapon, will be considered; his deployment of androgyny will be discussed, as well as his symbiotic interaction with urban space – especially New York – to sustain individuality and achieve, in his view, ordinariness. The chapter draws upon the written works of Crisp, extensive interviews with the man, and debates about representation and sexuality. The confounding of identity will be clarified with reference to the English culture which tried to mould, or mend, him. The apparently split sense of self will be elucidated by his own agency – his attempt to armour himself with ambiguity. Crisp both resisted dominant cultural norms and accommodated them. The chapter assesses his intrepid and idiosyncratic manner of coping with, and confronting, hostility to what he termed his "androgynous anarchy". It scrutinises the painful animosity he encountered from others for being different, and its interplay with the puzzling animosity he manifested, at times, towards himself.

Quentin Crisp burst through the cocoon of middle-class suburbia. Spreading his wings, he metamorphosed from naked civil servant – a poorly paid, anonymous artist's model – to become a well-dressed master of civility: - internationally "notorious", to use his own self-description (Q. Crisp, personal communication, June 1998), for his ambiguous sexual identity and for his witty way of exhibiting it. Crisp was happy to admit he was "a butterfly on the wheel" (Crisp, 1996, p. 18); he proved, however, considerably more durable (and sometimes more gaudily coloured) than the average butterfly.

Crisp seemed to attract two, as it were, camps. For his campest admirers, he was the queer Messiah figure of the 20th century, his cross was pink and massive, and he suffered persecution on a daily basis. With his policy of non-violent passive resistance, he almost became, to some adoring eyes, something of a gay Ghandi. This was the Crisp who, in his seventies, emigrated to a studio flat next to Hell's Angels in New York's East Village – at a time of life when some people emigrate as far as the local nursing home. This was the Crisp who defiantly declared his difference, despite the regular hate crimes inflicted upon him in pre-war Britain; the Crisp who, with the televised film about his life, helped domesticate camp for some viewers in a heterosexual audience. This was the Crisp considered chic enough to feature in Levi commercials, art-house films such as *Orlando* (Potter, 2002), Hollywood blockbusters like *Philadelphia* (Demme & Nyswaner, 1993). Few octogenarians would be thought sufficiently modish to feature in those anthems to anorexic youth, the Calvin Klein advertisements. Fewer still, in their ninetieth year, would expect to feature in the first controversial commercial with a homosexual theme on terrestrial British television, targeted at young women: Crisp's momentary presence in the Summer 1998 *Impulse* advertisement, aired frequently to a prime-time soap opera audience, confirmed his status as a master signifier of deviance.

A fascinating case study in confounded sexual identity, he was, for some, the elder statesman of sexual difference in the West. The benefit of great age, he told me, "is that one can overact appallingly" (Q. Crisp, personal communication, June 1998). This "stately homo of England", as he called himself, unknown for fifty years, became more significant for making a career out of his sexual singularity the older he became. He reversed the assumption that old age implies a slow, inevitable descent into invisibility and irrelevance; Crisp had never been more culturally visible, nor more culturally relevant.

To his critics, however, who have included lesbian and queer activists, Crisp was more traitor than martyr. This was evident in San Francisco, where one might have thought he would feel at home; yet, he admits, it "is the only place where I have received totally bad notices" (Q. Crisp, personal communication, June 1998). This was the Crisp who calls his sexuality his "problem"; the very first line of his autobiography is a telling indication of a confounded sexual identity: "I was so *disfigured* [italics

166

added] by the characteristics of a certain kind of homosexual person that, when I grew up, I realised that I could not ignore my predicament" (Crisp, 1968, p. 1). Crisp's somewhat eugenicist position surprised those who encountered him; he felt that his position was entirely consistent: "what did they expect me to say, when my autobiography begins as it does" (Q. Crisp, personal communication, June 1998).

His autobiography ends, too, on a note indicative of his complicated identity: "We think we write definitively of those parts of our nature that are dead and therefore beyond change, but that which writes is still changing – *still in doubt* [italics added] ... I stumble to my grave *confused* [italics added], and hurt and hungry" (Crisp, 1968, p. 217). This was the Crisp, his critics would point out, who called Aids a fad, who dismissed that other gay icon and victim figure, Princess Diana, as trash, who needed to shock. Crisp, for his detractors, represented an outmoded, if not offensive, way of resisting compulsory heterosexuality – a man whose sexuality was so confounded as not to be taken seriously.

This chapter does take Crisp, and his wit, seriously. It does not attempt to find some unhappy medium between his detractors and his apologists; rather, it seeks to explore what these antithetical reactions tell us about the contradictions within Crisp himself. It seeks to make sense of the semiotic warfare which this Princess of Queerness seemed to wage. To do this, it was necessary to interview the man. As Crisp was rather like a talking book, with an extraordinary tendency to quote himself, it was necessary to encourage him to comment on things he had not previously done. Surrounding himself in quotation marks, one had to consider whether the self he projected was a figment of his own fantasy, or a figment of one's own. As Richard Dyer pointed out to me at the time, for a man who had made his life a theatre, "getting to the truth about Quentin Crisp" was no easy task. Did Crisp mean what he said? Did he communicate his identity with arch aphorisms that he did not really mean? Or, as Dyer advised, "is there a third level?: he means what he actually says, but pretends not to" (Dyer, personal communication, 1998).

How did Crisp present himself at interview in his favourite bar? For a ninety year old, he was of unusually erect posture. He still wore his cravat, a faded velvet jacket and a green shirt, frayed at the collar. The cosmetics for which he was famous looked positively subtle compared to New York's brassier drag queens who stiletto-stalked the streets at the time of the interview (June, 1998); the mascara was barely visible; the cowboy hat looked particularly incongruous. He appeared, from a distance, strangely like a great grandmother. The voice was a distinctive warble, something like velvet dragged along gravel. The mannerisms were mildly theatrical.

In discussing his complicated sexual identity, one needs to address the fundamental mode of self-presentation which Crisp adopted: camp. Medhurst makes a useful preliminary point:

> ... camp – before it is anything else – before it gets scrutinised and squabbled over and splayed out on the operating table of theoretical analysis by academics like me – is part of gay men's daily lives, one of the ways in which they have managed to make sense of a world which at best tolerates and at worst exterminates them. (Medhurst, 1997, p. 51)

Crisp had his own definition: "Now [camp] means anything done not for the intrinsic value of the action, but

168

in order to demonstrate one's individuality in doing it – showing off" (Crisp, 1996, p. 196). Camp is this, and more than this. As Sontag suggested, camp is a way in which those of minority sexuality have sought to make some impression on the culture of the society in which they live. Mastery of style and wit has been a way of declaiming that gay and lesbian people have something distinctive to offer (Sontag, 1982). Camp has been recuperated into a postmodern queer discourse, and Crisp, with his self-invention, his love of ambiguous self-presentations and glittering surfaces, can be seen as a postmodern figure with a postmodern identity.

The humorous dimension of camp which Crisp deployed had a very serious purpose; it need not be conscious strategy to be an effective way of negotiating the revelation of self. It is also a shield from heterosexist hate crimes, a device to defuse hostility and win friends from a majority which, if it so desires, as it so often has, can crush or confound the sexual identity of a minority. If you are going to tell people the truth, George Bernard Shaw said, you had better make them laugh, or they will kill you (Q. Crisp, personal communication, June 1998). Crisp insisted on "telling the truth about himself", and seems to have taken Shaw's advice when it looked as if people could kill him; for example, in the Thames TV film of his life, *The Naked Civil Servant* (Gold & Mackie, 1975), Crisp was beaten up by a mob, punched in the teeth, kicked in the groin, and left like a broken bundle bleeding on to the concrete. He managed to get up, black-eyed, bruised-faced, and offered, airily, that "I seem to have offended you gentlemen in some way". They laughed; he walked away. Wit, in a situation of extreme uncertainty of audience response, won Crisp time to survive in a hostile urban environment. It gave him space to continue to express his sexual identity. A more physical retaliation, in view of his vulnerability and the asymmetrical forces so often ranged and raging against him, could have resulted in the destruction not only of his identity, but of himself. Unlike the cohorts of Stonewall drag queens who fought back with their fists, Crisp was often on his own; he fought back with the weaponry his identity afforded him – his discourse.

As he told me, "During my Edwardian youth and Georgian middle age, the world stayed exactly where it was, aggressively conformist and conservative; I stayed exactly where I was, a blithe spirit revelling in androgynous anarchy, and there was a battle" (Q. Crisp, personal communication, June 1998). The battle was also internal. His identity was also a frustrated identity; it was androgynous anarchy, not least because, as he told me, he would have preferred to have had a sex change operation before the age of 25 if one had been available – but it was not (Q. Crisp, personal communication, June 1998). This was an admission he had never made before. It indicated that Crisp felt caught between what he was, and what he wanted to be. The confounding of his identity could stem, in part, based on this oral history, from a frustrated transsexuality.

Crisp, though troubled by his own gender, created the subversive possibilities for gender trouble; his dissident sexual acting-up seemed to transcend, or challenge, old binary restrictions, such as the male versus female polarity. The panoply of sexual actions which happen outside of heterosexual communities obviously cannot overthrow dominant heterocentric discourses; they can, however, at least disrupt them, if only momentarily, "through hyperbole, dissonance, internal confusion and proliferation"[1] (Butler, 1990, p. 31).

---

[1] However, there are qualifications to Butler's popular assertions, one

To continue to dye his hair red, paint himself with cosmetics more gaudily than many women then did, and parade his queerness as visibly as possible – without all the support structures and laws, however inadequate, in place now – was an act of resistance. Such dogged resistance is underestimated by those who dismiss him as an effete old queen. This effete old queen, roughed about for being rouged up, exhibited rather more courage than his persecutors. Camp may be thought of as a passive way of communicating sexual identity; articulated in front of a violently homophobic audience, it can be an act of decided *assertiveness*. To persist in displaying your identity, and to do it with a joke, in the knowledge that you may be corporally punished for it, demands a resilient sense of self of a very high order. It is a flourishing of sexual identity which confounds enemies. Every joke may not quite be a tiny revolution, but there is a subversive element to the

---

problem stemming from heterosexual incorporation of queer repertoires, the second from a heterosexist "backlash" against them. In either case, queer raids on straight society can be shrugged off. First, Butler's sweeping assertion that dissident acts are bound to weaken heterosexual discourses seems rather optimistic; heterosexual power is rather more entrenched than she seems to suggest. Dominant culture is not necessarily enfeebled by deviant figures who may, in time, become domesticated and welcomed into heterosociety. This incorporation happened in Crisp's later years – evidenced, for example, by the fact that *Resident Alien* was a best-seller. An alternative challenge to Butler's generalisations is that dissident sexual response, far from weakening them, can unleash a snarling reassertion of heterosexual discourses; this can lead to attempts to weaken, or even wipe out, queer expressions. This backlash happened to Crisp in his earlier years: "by constituting myself the one among the many, I had provoked the worst behaviour in others ... this wrought no change whatever in the character of my enemies, but caused the disintegration of my own" (Q. Crisp, personal communication, June 1998). This, then, adds weight to the idea that his sexuality was confounded owing to the internal damage inflicted by the regular physical and mental attacks upon him.

defiantly witty mode of camp. That subversive possibility should not be exaggerated, and nor should it be erased. In a typically insightful article on camp in general, Dyer pointed out:

> You've only got to think of the impact of Quentin Crisp's high camp ... on the straight world he came up against, to see that camp has a radical/progressive potential: scaring muggers who know that all this butch male bit is not really them but who feel they have to act as if it is (Quentin showed that he knew they were screamers underneath it all); running rings of logic and wit round the pedestrian ideas of psychiatrists, magistrates and the rest; and developing by living out a high camp lifestyle a serenity and a sense of being at-one-with-yourself .... (Dyer, 1992, p. 135)

Crisp had his debt to other queers known for using camp and wit in a coded way of, if not always revealing sexual identity, at least hinting at it. Although he was surprisingly dismissive toward Wilde, labelling him as "sordid" (Q. Crisp, personal communication, June 1998), they are connected in queer lineage. Both suffered for, and gained inspiration from, their sexual identity, using humorous discourse to negotiate their way around anti-homosexual prejudice. Both achieved notoriety as a result of distinctive self-stylisation in their prose and manner of living, style marinated in their sexuality – queerness was always implied in their work, even if not overtly stated. There were nuances to their sexual identity; when the state perceived their identity had moved from ambiguity, or implication, to actualisation of sexuality, then, in moral panic, it sought to discipline and punish it. Queer linguistic play earned toleration, for it gave heterosexual audiences cultural pleasure; the suspicion of queer genital play brought about attempted termination, for it gave homosexual protagonists pleasure. Well before there was a Red Scare, there was an under-acknowledged Pink Scare. Both men were put on trial by the state for, at root, the expression of sexual dissidence. Resisting this attempt at juridical sexual cleansing, both again deployed wit to win, if nothing else, the approval of the gallery. Both seemed to have a degree of confounded sexual identity: Wilde, who could speak so eloquently about most things, would not dare to speak the name of his love; Crisp, bafflingly, dared to stigmatise the sexuality he did so much to publicise. Crisp's self-definition as "exhibitionist and martyr" (Q. Crisp, personal communication, June 1998), at least unconsciously, owed something to the Wildean inheritance. These men made their own sexual history, but certainly not in circumstances of their choosing.

Crisp's stylised sexual identity had, therefore, more of a connection to the Wildean legacy than he would have cared to admit. Camp originates from queer hopes of imitating the taste and behavioural codes of aristocrats, a lineage emanating from the aftermath of the Wilde trial. As Sinfield argues, the Wilde image was influential in developing a connection between class and camp which ripples through gay ghettoes a century later; much queer campery, such as "Crisperanto", whether conscious or subconscious, holds "a lurking recollection of the effeminate leisure-class dandy" (Sinfield, 1994, p. 156). Crisp's feminine appearance, his advice "never to work" and to live off "champagne and peanuts" at parties, his admission that he did "nothing" and often remained indoors, inert in his dressing gown, for two days a week (Q. Crisp, personal communication, June 1998), underlined Sinfield's argument. Like Beau Brummell, he defined himself, when outdoors, by showy cravats and outré hats. If one was to describe him as a dandy, it would be useful to find a definition:

> [The dandy] is a man whose office and existence consists in the wearing of clothes. Every faculty of his soul, spirit, purse and person is heroically consecrated to the wearing of clothes wisely and well so that, as others dress to live, he lives to dress. But look at him and he is content. (Crisp, 1988, p. 8)

Crisp's identity was more complicated than that; nonetheless, a facet of his sexual identity was advertised via the adorned body.

Whilst Crisp may have been subconsciously indebted to previous queer icons, queer entertainers, perhaps queer "communities", too, have a debt to him. Crisp was a link in the queer lineage between the witty discourse of Wilde and the dragged-up street fighting of Stonewall; fittingly, his autobiography came out the year before the riot in Christopher Street. His use of wit to give his identity safe passage in society put him in the line of English gay comics who have managed to tickle the feet of the heterosexual giant whilst under its shadow: Kenneth Williams, Larry Grayson, John Inman and Julian Clary, for example, owe something to the *social* coming out of homosexuality which Crisp helped to bring about. He shunned the idea of "a cause", even though he was a leading player in publicising queerness and rendering it, eventually, a little more acceptable to straight society. Sharing queer stories in the face of a frowning world was, as Edmund White says, a key step in shaping future developments, "forging an identity as much as revealing it" (White, 1991, p. 1).

Coming out as a personal issue for Crisp was less relevant; he was never "in". He was criticised by an audience in San Francisco for not stating during his performance that he was gay: "I would have thought that would have been obvious enough by my appearance" (Q. Crisp, personal communication, June 1998). Hence, the simple binary of "in" or "out" is not one he himself would have recognised in the production of his identity. Revelation of sexuality tends not to be a one-off moment; as, in most environments, people tend to assume an individual is heterosexual, "coming out" is a potentially endless process. Crisp subverted expectation and shortened the process of disclosure by his immediately deviant appearance; hence he revealed, or at least implied, his sexuality initially by dress, rather than discourse.

How would Crisp have defined his sexual identity? There is always presumption in speaking for others, and Crisp should be given space to speak for himself. For him:

> Most people are content to cherish their mere identity. This is not
>
> enough. Our identity is just a group of ill-assorted characteristics
>
> that we happen to be born with. Like our fingerprints, if they are
>
> noticed at all, they will certainly be used against us. (Crisp, 1996, p.
>
> 4)

Crisp's assumption that identity can be used against you surely emanated from the regular beatings he received. The physical punishment must have left its psychical scars; it is perhaps these which explain his need simultaneously to display his identity and to damn it – that paradox which leads one to frame his identity as confounded. Similarly, the revulsion he seems to have had for the act of gay sex may in part result from the sordid experiences he received at the hands and genitals of men in dark alleys to whom he sold sex as a young man. Never having addressed the issue of oral sex, for example, he shuddered with horror as he gasped, "Who would want to put a man's penis in his mouth?" (Q. Crisp, personal communication, June 1998). His castigation of the homosexual's life as "horrible", his sweeping assertion that "all homosexual men spend all their days in public lavatories, and all their nights behind questionable bars" (Q. Crisp, personal communication, June 1998), reflects a fossilised world view; there were more limited openings for queer expression for much of Crisp's life. His responses were both conditioned by his own unsatisfactory early experiences and, no doubt, a need to generate comment. Bold comment brings attention, and it was attention, ideally *benign* attention, that this exhibitionist needed. Crisp pointed out:

> People have always imagined, or pretended to imagine that I seek to provoke hostile attention. That is rubbish. What I want is to be accepted by other people without bevelling down my individuality to please them – because if I do that, all the attention, all the friendship, all the hospitality I receive is really for somebody else of the same name. I want love on my own terms. (Crisp, 1996, p. 8)

Perhaps it is no wonder he said that homosexuals "stand on the bank, watching the real people swim" (Q. Crisp, personal communication, June 1998) when, for most of his life, his sexuality was illegal, classified as a perversion by the army and much of the society that he tried to join. No theory of sexuality, as Weeks (1985, p. 180) points out, is complete which fails to learn the lessons of the unconscious. In the dialectical tension between Crisp's internalisation of homophobia and his insistence upon expressing it, his complicated identity, perhaps, can be located. This tension, on the inside, seemed to run through the subconscious and was expressed, on the outside, by his contradictory actions. "Seems" is a necessary qualification, for we cannot, of course, measure the subconscious mathematically. As a critic unqualified in psychiatry, however, I can at least modestly assert that, if repressed English society had told him he was inferior for so long and for so often, part of Crisp's psyche absorbed that, even as part of him decided to rebel against it. Eros and Thanatos were fighting it out in the Crisp consciousness; the schizophrenic self-display and self-negation resulted.

For Crisp, the act of sex was less important to his identity than his individual lifestyle. Revolted by gay sex and celibate for many years, his self-expression had been sublimated in the aestheticisation of everyday life. He had learnt to market that distinctiveness in order to win favour from the heterosexual dictatorship:

> You have to polish up your raw identity into a lifestyle so that you
> can barter with the outside world for what you want. The polishing
> process makes your life so formal that, by comparison, the life of a
> Trappist monk is an orgy. The search for a lifestyle involves a
> journey to the interior. This is not altogether a pleasant experience,
> because you not only have to take stock of what you consider to be
> your assets, but also have to take a long look at what your friends
> call "the trouble with you". Nevertheless, the journey is worth
> making. Indeed, we might say that the whole purpose of existence
> is to reconcile the glowing opinion we have of ourselves with the
> terrible things other people say about us. (Crisp, 1996, p. 4)

His sexual identity was, then, in a sense, *asexual*. This was part of his complicated identity; it raised the question: why invest so much energy in deviant self-presentation, if one is to shun the fulfilment of that deviance? "I am not a practising homosexual", he said; "I am already perfect" (Q. Crisp, personal communication, June 1998). Witticism aside, the absence of sex from his life made him a less threatening figure to heterosexual society; that, combined with the vulnerability of age and softening social mores, ushered in gradual acceptance by mainstream society, especially after the widely-seen television film version of *The Naked Civil Servant* (Gold & Mackie, 1975): "they could see I wasn't doing any harm" (Q. Crisp, personal communication, June 1998). Harm, on the contrary, was done to him. Crisp's asexuality, along with his wit, was part of a gentle strategy of neutralising opposition – a form of non-violent resistance. His celibate image was underlined by his role as Elizabeth the First in Sally Potter's film, *Orlando* (2002). The Queen presented herself as an illusory figure, constructing her own famed identity and mythical status around her chasteness. Nicknamed the Virgin Queen, musicians, poets and playwrights of the day exploited this to the full, perpetuating the image which lingers. Crisp originally survived by using his body for money when young; when old, he, like the Queen, built an identity on containing and decorating his body and, like her, was perceived by heterosexual communities as an asexual figure (Russo, 1994).

Crisp was able not only to reveal, but also revel, in his asexual identity by emigrating to the urban space of New York. The city meant that life began at 70 for him – it became his haven. Unlike in the London of his youth and middle age, Crisp was never attacked or even verbally abused in the street; instead, as I witnessed, people came up to him, often smiled and greeted him. The greatest harassment, he recalled, came from an overly concerned Puerto Rican lady who tried to send him to hospital against his will and bundled him into an ambulance. This was not simply because New York, with its vibrant queer community which, as of 1998, stretched from Greenwich Village through to Chelsea, constituting up to 20% of the population, was a more conducive environment for queerness; the records of the Gay and Lesbian Anti-Violence Project (personal communication, 1998) indicate that gay New Yorkers often suffered verbal or physical violence. It was the gentleness and friendliness of Crisp's identity which was mirrored in the reactions of others. It was, too, the celebrity status; he was part of a gay gerontocracy. It has been claimed that, on any person who desires such queer prizes, New York will bestow the gift of loneliness and the gift of privacy. Yet Crisp was never lonely in the city; people called him and visited regularly – he received 200 emails a week, becoming an electronic Agony Uncle. Nor was his life especially private. Wherever he went, he was noticed. His public self was always on display. The dirty dandy was unusual in presenting his theatrical self so consistently. In New York, a network of supporters, often drag queens, assisted him if he injured himself. Confirming his acceptance by society and iconic status within the city, he was measured for a waxwork for the new Madame Tussauds in Times Square. Manhattan took this master of masquerade to its bosom, the polar opposite of pre-War London, which left him out in the cold. Wilde worried that he might be entering an open prison for the insane when he entered New York; he soon claimed its inhabitants to be thoroughly charming. Crisp, before his silver-tipped cane even first scraped an East Village sidewalk, never had any doubts that they would be otherwise.

New York is a city that befits the eccentricity which was a key part of the Crispean identity. As Simmel (1950) pointed out, individuals are tempted to adopt the most tendentious peculiarities, specifically metropolitan extravagances of mannerism, caprice and preciousness.

Implicit here is the notion of arbitrariness: the city is so large, so amorphous, that eccentricity can function as a sign of uniqueness. Hence, Crisp's strange hat that he wore, "rather like one Clint Eastwood once wore", he declared, half-jokingly (Q. Crisp, personal communication, June 1998), was a sign of his distinctive identity, which did not look out of place in Manhattan. In a city thriving on eccentricity, it is difficult to locate a stable definition of normal identity.

"There is an unalterable law", Crisp contended, "that states all of society's outsiders must live in big cities" (Q. Crisp, personal communication, June 1998). Crisp felt at home in New York: "I was always American at heart" (Q. Crisp, personal communication, June 1998). The heart of his identity was finally freed in the East Village. As Mencken wrote, "New York is not all bricks and steel. There are hearts there too, and if they do not break, then at least they know how to leap" (Mencken, 1990, p. 417). For Crisp, one should not underestimate the sense of miracle that it represented for him to be able simply to be himself in safety. It was a place for him to parade his identity and to watch others, safely, as he stared out from his favourite diner or strolled down Manhattan streets carried by the rhythms of the city. Although he was not incognito, to a limited degree Crisp otherwise recalled Baudelaire's flâneur:

> ... for the perfect flâneur, for the passionate spectator, it is an immense joy to set up house in the heart of the multitude, amid the ebb and flow of movement, in the midst of the fugitive and the infinite, to be away from home and yet to feel oneself everywhere at home; to see the world, to be at the centre of the world.... (Baudelaire, 1964, p. 9)

Crisp watched the world whilst it watched him; he was a performer, keenly watching the theatre of the street around him as he participated in it.

Manhattan afforded Crisp the ability to live what can be called a carnival life, as people perpetually reacted to his identity in a benign, often enthusiastic manner. The Russian critic Bakhtin pointed out that, in the Middle Ages, there was no division between performers and spectators: "Carnival is not contemplated and strictly speaking, not even performed; its participants live in it, they live by its laws as long as those laws are in effect; that is, they live a carnivalistic life" (Bakhtin, 1984, p. 34) In carnival, what is suspended is hierarchical structure ... everything resulting from socio-historical inequality or any other form of inequality among people (including age): "distance between people is suspended, and a special carnival category goes into effect; ... free and familiar contact among people" (Bakhtin, p. 34). Certainly, in illustration of the absence of distance in response to his identity, complete strangers came up to Crisp and engaged him in conversation as if they knew him. He made himself freely available by listing his number in the telephone book; he could be accessed via email and was deluged by messages, and he had his own website, managed by guardian angels, lit up by Warhol-style repetitions of his facial image. The contact was so free and familiar that he was even rung up at 7.30 in the morning by a woman wanting to know how to apply lipstick without it smearing. From being spat at for his ambiguous identity, he became consulted as a guru of queerness. It was a remarkable transformation in reception to him, with his life representing one of those rare things outside Hollywood – a seemingly happy ending.

Carnival functions as a dress rehearsal for better times;

reception of Crisp's identity gave us a glimpse of how diverse sexual identity may one day be more widely accepted. It allows the latent sides of human nature to reveal and express themselves (Bakhtin, 1984). Crisp had previously had only the rarest glimpses of the carnival life, when he descended into wartime Portsmouth, where he was surrounded by a posse of sailors, who flirted with him on the seafront: "the first, last and only time that I ever sat in a crowd of people whose attention I really desired without once feeling I was in danger" (Q. Crisp, personal communication, June 1998). Until, that is, he reached New York, where this moment of safety became a more permanent process. Crisp himself used the idea of carnival to describe his experience of safety and spectacle and desire in urban space: "the whole town was like a vast carnival" (Crisp, 1968, p. 97). Carnival helps to lower barriers as much as inhibitions.

Carnival helps fuse together "the sacred with the profane, the lofty with the low, the great with the insignificant, the wise with the stupid" (Bakhtin, 1984, p. 10). Crisp talked to anybody, and anybody would talk to him. He tried to look like an aristocrat, influenced perhaps by grand English society queens like Stephen Tennant; yet he lived a meagre existence in one room in a poor part of Manhattan. He resided next to Hells Angels and, sometimes, cockroaches, amongst the nadir of the metropolis; yet he hobnobbed with professors, film directors, and the elites of Manhattan.

A facet of the carnivalesque life, often misunderstood, as Bakhtin (1984, p. 34) points out, is the mock crowning and decrowning of a king. This does not eulogise the office of kingship, but the "joyful relativity" of transformation. It is the "shift itself, the very process of replaceability, and not the precise item that is replaced". Crisp played, and was associated with, the idea of the regal in a manner that recalls Bakhtin's carnival. He was featured in a special Channel 4 programme delivering an "Alternative Queen's Speech" (Crisp, 1983, December 25). Even Crisp's email address began "HRH QCrisp". Famously, of course, he played Elizabeth the First in the film *Orlando* (Potter, 2002), in which the relativity of transformation is celebrated. The ambiguous presentation of sexuality and the relativity of and reincarnation of sexuality are finely delineated in the film. Crisp's role as Elizabeth spans both the birth and death of the Orlando figure; the use of a feminine man to play Elizabeth underlines the idea of replaceable bodies, of how a man can "be" a woman, and of confusing bodies – how one may not always be quite sure which is which. Crisp undermined the idea of fixity in gender. Carnival laughter includes ridicule wrapped up with rejoicing; it articulates a view of the world in antithesis to the monolithically serious view of officialdom forces. Carnival temporarily refuses the official world (Bakhtin, 1984). Crisp beguiled the court and his critics by wit, with which they could not cope – the well-aimed slingshot at Goliath. He sent up every societal restriction that others attempted to strap around him. When accused of "suffering" from sexual perversion, he said "glorying" would be a better description (Q. Crisp, personal communication, June 1998). When the Army doubted whether or not he had a fantasy vision of himself as a fighting man, he pointed out his qualifications were ample: "anyone can get killed" (Gold & Mackie, 1975). People could not handle him, so they manhandled him. Crisp again embraced some of Bakhtin's (1984) idea, embracing the strands of laughter, the profane, the unofficial, the open and the contingent, which make up carnivalesque life – the carnivalesque identity.

Conclusion

Crisp negotiated a revelation of self, the sexual expression of which, for much of his life, was policed and punished. In confounding his enemies by persisting in his sexual identity, he contributed to confounding that identity – subconsciously absorbing the idea that homosexuality was inferior. As the sun went down on this dandy's life, there were signs that he was a little less confused about himself, as people grew to be a little less confused about, and much more accepting of, him. Illustrating the point, as my interview with him ended, a police car rolled up; a stern-looking officer beckoned Crisp with his finger. The pensioner tottered over and, leaning on his umbrella, enquired, "Have I done anything illegal?". "No", the officer replied, grinning, "we just wondered how the show was going." In a moment, that little incident seemed to encapsulate a revolution in attitudes to sexual identity within Crisp's lifetime; a revolution which he played his own micro part in generating. Crisp's show was one of the longest running in town; it played for decades. As one of the more invincible homosexuals of modern times turned and waved goodbye, silhouetted by a faintly pink dusk, I realised the importance, and the impertinence, of being Quentin.

If this was a butterfly on the wheel, as he called himself, it was one with steel wings. Those wings carried him through all the cultural resistance which tried to clip his identity, and flew him into warmer climes. People used to laugh at him; in the end they laughed *with* him. A universe can be reflected in a preposition. He functioned as one of the acid tests (out of many such tests) of cultural responses to sexual ambiguity, as expressed by a Western celebrity in a particular time and locale. In more recent and happier years, cultural accommodation of Crisp's identity was a sign of hope, a sign that dissident sexual identities stood more of a chance, though no safe passage can ever be guaranteed. As the Reverend Peter Gomes put it:

> ... the place for creative hope that arises out of suffering most likely now is to be found among blacks, women, and homosexuals. These outcasts may well be the custodians of those thin places; they may in fact be the watchers at the frontier between what is and what is to be. (Gomes, 1998, p. 230)

Crisp summed up his identity by claiming that he was in "the profession of being" (Q. Crisp, personal communication, June 1998). There can be no more fitting words, then, than those of Sting, who wrote of this Englishman in New York:

> takes a man to suffer ignorance and smile
>
> he's the hero of the hour ...
>
> Be yourself, no matter what they say. (Sting, 1987)

Whatever your identity, and however confounded that identity, insistently being yourself, the Crispean example suggested, was one way to confound the enemies of sexual difference.

It was, however, still a problematic way of being in the world, when the quintessence of Crisp, as this chapter attempts to show, appeared to flee from its set of selves, as much as, in other moments, it sought to embrace them. Being himself, as Sting put it, or rather, being his selves, was not an easy nor always a heroic matter for Quentin as he performed his masquerade.

Crisp was, in the last analysis, hardly a role model cleansed of blemish; instead, he attained a dignified, if fractured, deviance – ambiguity, self-negation, self-publicity, wit, bravery and prejudice. Yet, despite an identity riddled with contradictions, his admirers recognised that his celebrity and eccentricity were a negotiated, hard-won achievement, whilst his detractors were far away, leading drabber lives that no one wrote about when they lived or when they expired; in fact, it might have been difficult to tell the difference. Quentin was, then, a rather cracked artefact (or arty fact), though no less intriguing for all the cracks; however dusty that antiquated, guilt-edged image may become in culture, there should always be quite a few bidders at auction for this original work of art in a bent and broken frame.

References

Bakhtin. M. M. (1984). *Problems of Dostoevsky's poetics* (C. Emerson, Ed. & Trans.). Manchester: Manchester University Press. (Original work published 1929).

Baudelaire, C. (1964). *The painter of modern life, and other essays* (J. Mayne, Trans.). Oxford: Phaidon.

Butler, J. (1990). *Gender trouble: Feminism and the subversion of identity.* New York: Routledge.

Crisp, Q. (1968). *The naked civil servant.* London: Jonathan Cape.

Crisp, Q. (1983, December 25). *The alternative Queen's speech* [Television broadcast]. London: Channel 4.

Crisp, Q. (1984). *The wit and wisdom of Quentin Crisp* (G.

Kettelhack, Ed.). New York: Harper & Row.

Crisp, Q. (1988). Preface. In J. B. d'Aurevilly, *Dandyism* (D. Ainslie, Trans.). New York: PAJ Publications.

Crisp, Q. (1996). *Resident alien: The New York diaries* (D. Carroll, Ed.). London: HarperCollins.

Demme, J. (Director), & Nyswaner, R. (Writer). (1993). *Philadelphia* [Motion picture]. United States: Clinica Estetico; United States: TriStar Pictures.

Dyer, R. (1992). It's being so camp as keeps us going. In R. Dyer, *Only entertainment* (pp. 135-147). London: Routledge.

Gold, J. (Director), & Mackie, P. (Writer). (1975). *The naked civil servant* [Television motion picture]. United Kingdom: Thames Television.

Gomes, P. J. (1998). *The good book: Reading the Bible with mind and heart.* (New ed.). New York: Avon Books. (Original ed. published 1996).

Medhurst, A. (1997). Camp. In A. Medhurst & S. R. Munt, (Eds.), *Lesbian and gay studies: A critical introduction* (pp. 274-293). London, Cassell.

Mencken, H. L. (1990). There are parts for all in the "Totentanz". In A. Klein, (Ed.), *Empire city: A treasury of New York* (pp. 416-420). (New ed.) Salem, NH: Ayer.

(This essay originally published, 1927).

Potter, S. (Writer/Director). (2002). *Orlando* [Motion picture]. United Kingdom: Adventure Pictures.

Russo, M. (1994). *The female grotesque: Risk, excess and modernity.* New York: Routledge.

Simmel, G. (1950). The metropolis and mental life. In G. Simmel, *The sociology of Georg Simmel* (K. H. Wolff, Trans. & Ed.) (pp. 409-24). New York: Free Press. (Original work published 1903).

Sinfield, A. (1994). *The Wilde century: Effeminacy, Oscar Wilde and the queer moment.* London: Cassell.

Sontag, S. (1982). *A Susan Sontag reader.* Harmondsworth: Penguin.

Sting (1987). Englishman in New York. On *Nothing like the sun* [Record]. Hollywood: A&M Records.

Weeks, J. (1985). *Sexuality and its discontent*s: *Meanings, myths and modern sexualities.* London: Routledge & Kegan Paul.

White, E. (1991). *The Faber book of gay short fiction.* London: Faber and Faber.